# POWER
## — IN THE —
# BLOOD

# POWER
## — IN THE —
# BLOOD

### CLAIMING YOUR SPIRITUAL
### INHERITANCE

## SANDIE FREED

**Chosen**
*a division of Baker Publishing Group*
Minneapolis, Minnesota

Previously published under the title *Strategies from Heaven's Throne*

Published by Chosen Books
11400 Hampshire Avenue South
Bloomington, Minnesota 55438
www.chosenbooks.com

Chosen Books is a division of
Baker Publishing Group, Grand Rapids, Michigan

Printed in the United States of America

Library of Congress Cataloging-in-Publication Data

Freed, Sandie.
    Power in the blood : claiming your spiritual inheritance / Sandie Freed ; foreword by Bill Hamon.
        p.   cm.
    Summary : "When believers realize they are royalty through Jesus' shed blood, they can discover their full spiritual inheritance, including eternal life, identity, authority, destiny, and more"—Provided by publisher.
    Rev. ed. of: Strategies from heaven's throne.
    ISBN 978-0-8007-9551-1 (pbk. : alk. paper)
    1. Christian life. I. Freed, Sandie, date— Strategies from heaven's throne. II. Title.
BV4501.3.F737 2013
248.4—dc23
                                                    2012034620

Cover design by Kirk DouPonce, DogEared Design

13   14   15   16   17   18   19        7   6   5   4   3   2   1

This book is dedicated to the Lord Jesus Christ,
the Lamb who shed His blood for all mankind.
His sacrifice at the Cross has provided an
eternal reward and a divine inheritance.
Yes, there is "power in the blood"!

# CONTENTS

Foreword by Dr. Bill Hamon    9

Introduction    11

1. Dancing with the King    21
2. The Blood and the Atonement    33
3. The Blood Covenant and Our Inheritance    41
4. The Highway of Holiness    61
5. We Need to See!    79
6. Resisting Religious Paradigms    107
7. Every Knee Must Bow    131
8. Coming Out of the Wilderness    143
9. Crossing Over into the Promised Land    157
10. Our Spiritual Weapons    178
11. Hidden in Christ    189
12. Establishing Your Victory Structure    203

# fOREWORD

Sandie has made a tremendous contribution to the Body of Christ. In this book, you will learn how to discover the hindrances that keep you from possessing your full inheritance in Christ Jesus. The truths and principles presented will empower you to leave your wilderness, cross over your Jordan and enter into your promised land of blessing and prophetic fulfillment.

I have been fully knowledgeable of Sandie's life, family and ministry for nearly twenty years. I can assure you that the truths presented here were not just gleaned from reading a book. They are truths that have been proven by living and practicing them in her daily life and ministry.

Sandie keeps the flow of her book interesting by presenting many visions and personal experiences. As you read, you will gain insight concerning how to fulfill the scriptural command to go from glory to glory until you are conformed to the image of Christ and fulfill your ministry destiny.

This book will give you great enlightenment and encouragement, as it will to Christians around the world. As children of God, we are made joint heirs with Christ Jesus, who promised those who overcome all things the right to sit down with Him on His Father's throne. This means that we have throne room rights and authority. To appropriate and exercise these throne room rights, we need strategies from heaven's throne. God bless you, Sandie, for taking the time and effort to put these truths into a book. Because of it, many Christians will be blessed and move forward in their journey of fulfilling their calling and ministry in Christ Jesus.

Dr. Bill Hamon, founder of
Christian International Ministries and
author of nine books, including *Day of the Saints*

# INTRODUCTION

Of all the twelve tribes of Israel, one tribe was ordained and destined to understand the times and seasons—the tribe of Issachar. Issachar was the ninth son of Jacob and the fifth by his wife Leah. One translation of his name is "one to be rewarded." The Scripture describes the sons of Issachar as those who "understood the times and knew what Israel should do" (1 Chronicles 12:32).

Today we believers are being rewarded with an Issachar anointing. As sons of Issachar, we have the very same ability to understand the times in which we live and to know what to do! And, along with that truth, is the present-day revelation of knowing that *each of us has a spiritual inheritance to claim and possess.* Our inheritance is given those who have received Jesus as their Lord and Savior. We are sons and daughters in God and, therefore, have an inheritance.

I will explain more on that as we travel along, but for now just think of yourself as being a *King's* kid with an inheritance connected to the Kingdom governed by a King. (Of course I am referring to the King of kings and His Kingdom.) If you can imagine the lavish royal benefits that are usually connected to a king and his kingdom, you will understand better this journey we take together. In fact, chapter 1 begins with a dream God gave me that concerns dancing with the King. You are going to be filled with hope and joy as you read what God has in store for each of us who are believers in Christ.

It is very important to understand the connection between the title of this book and its subtitle. If you grasp this now and keep it in the front of your mind as you move from chapter to chapter, you will receive greater revelation. Ponder the title and subtitle: *Power in the Blood: Claiming Your Spiritual Inheritance.* This is rich with meaning.

Pairing the shed *blood* of Jesus, the King of kings, with our subsequent *inheritance* gives the basis for our royal lineage. Think of how we refer to royalty as having "royal blood" and "a rich bloodline" and "pure lineage." Royals prize "uncontaminated" blood, choosing to pass their legacies from generation to generation through the flow of it. Many of us today are researching our *family* trees and tracing our lineages through bloodlines. Finding who we are based on whose blood we have flowing in our earthly veins is important, right? Just think how much more important it is for us to have access to the power of the blood of Jesus and understand how that blood empowers us today to claim our full inheritance.

Inheritance can only be claimed by proving legal blood relationship or heirship. You have chosen the perfect study if you desire to claim your inheritance through Christ Jesus. You will learn that the two concepts of power in His blood and claiming your inheritance tie together perfectly.

Many of us recall that beloved hymn "There Is Power in the Blood" (written by Lewis E. Jones in 1899). Read or sing it and note the words I have italicized, words that relate to power, victory and freedom due to the blood of the King:

Would you be *free* from the burden of sin?
There's *pow'r* in the blood, *pow'r* in the blood;
Would you o'er evil a *victory* win?
There's wonderful *pow'r* in the blood.

*Refrain*

There is pow'r, pow'r, wonder-working pow'r
In the blood of the Lamb;
There is pow'r, pow'r, wonder-working pow'r
In the precious blood of the Lamb.

Would you be *free* from your passion and pride?
There's *pow'r* in the blood, *pow'r* in the blood;
Come for a cleansing to Calvary's tide;
There's wonderful *pow'r* in the blood. [Refrain]

Would you be whiter, much whiter than snow?
There's *pow'r* in the blood, *pow'r* in the blood;
Sin-stains are lost in its life-giving flow;
There's wonderful *pow'r* in the blood. [Refrain]

Would you do service for *Jesus your King?*
There's *pow'r* in the blood, *pow'r* in the blood;
Would you live daily His praises to sing?
There's wonderful *pow'r* in the blood. [Refrain]

It is my heartfelt desire to share the revelation concerning what is promised to us by God, and, then, to show you how to claim and possess those promises. Again, this is all part of our royal inheritance. The key ingredient here is the blood.

## When the Thief Comes

At the same time, while many of us are gaining understanding of our times and seasons and learning how the Lord directs during those periods, we need to understand the spiritual battles with demonic forces that will attempt to hinder our breakthroughs and victories. There is a thief who is always ready to steal, kill and destroy (see John 10:10). We need fresh strategies in this season to ensure that we respond properly to the directions the Lord gives concerning victory in our spiritual battles.

Keep in mind as you read this book that Satan (and his many cohorts, which we will discuss along the way) will attempt to abort your destiny and steal your royal inheritance. We will stop periodically and examine our hearts, take time for repentance and receive a fresh empowerment from the Lord to continue advancing. I will be giving you many strategies and opportunities to gain confidence that you are indeed defeating the enemy's plans. Precious one, I desire that you walk in complete victory. I want you to receive your royal inheritance and walk in power.

What do I mean by strategies? A *strategy* is, first, "a plan or method of achieving a specific goal." *Webster's* dictionary also defines it as "the use of a stratagem" and "the art of planning and directing large-scale military movement and operation."

Most Christians understand that we are God's army. We are aware that we have an enemy, Satan. We understand our spiritual authority and, therefore, exercise dominion over the powers of darkness. Being seated with Christ in heavenly places gives us a "throne" of authority (see Ephesians 2:6). We need, however, to remain continually before *His* throne in order to receive fresh strategies for the battles we face today. It is important that you continually *see* yourself approaching the throne of God—*boldly*—as His child receiving fresh grace for whatever is needed to possess your inheritance—your *royal* inheritance. You will not be able to defeat the enemy in your own strength; therefore, we will closely examine God's throne of grace so that you can remain positioned for breakthroughs. We cannot fight today's battles with yesterday's victories. Each day is a new challenge, and we need life-sustaining infusions of the blood of Jesus to empower us for the battles that lie ahead.

*Strategy* is also defined as "having a stratagem," which is "a scheme or trick for surprising or deceiving an enemy." Dear one, the enemy has deceived us long enough. Yes, he is the *master schemer*, but can you agree with me that it is time to be wise as serpents and gain strategies to deceive him and thwart his plans? Heavenly strategies help us outthink and outsmart the devil!

## Isaiah Gained Strategy in the Throne Room

The prophet Isaiah received strategies from heaven's throne. In Isaiah 6, the prophet describes how he found himself before God's throne and what occurred there. Through this account, we learn several things about approaching the throne.

First, King Uzziah had to die before the prophet could fully witness God's glory. Isaiah experienced the death of "an old thing" and in that same season was finally able to see the "Lord seated on a throne, high and exalted" (Isaiah 6:1). Wow! Imagine that.

What has to die in us before we are able to embrace a throne room experience, to gain further understanding of God's glory and receive our inheritance? I used to believe that God wanted to strip me of all my dreams in order to test my heart and faithfulness toward Him. I now realize that God wants to bless me. He is always ready to resurrect our dreams—especially those that were stolen due to pain or trauma. I believe with my entire heart that God wants to fulfill our desires, but to do so *His way*. In other words, if we attempt to fulfill our destiny in Christ through our own methods—that is, control, manipulation, selfish gain—God will put His finger on it and then we have to die to our own manipulative measures.

Death to an old season is difficult. And, yes, it is necessary to let go of the past in order to move forward into our destiny. King Uzziah had to die before Isaiah could *see* the Lord. I believe that this, to a degree, resembled death to an old governmental structure. Old "kings" (I also refer to these as "strongholds") of our lives and their governmental control have to die for us fully to embrace *God's* government in our lives.

This does not mean that we should take up a martyr syndrome. On the contrary, we are in a season in which to shift out from legalism and limited thinking. You may be wondering what *limited thinking* is. *Limited thinking* is "any type of belief systems that short-circuits our ability to hear God and move forward with faith." Many times we have to let the old thing die so we can receive His life. Only then are we really able to see God high and lifted up—above our situations and circumstances.

Isaiah shifted into a new place full of God's glory. He witnessed throne-room life. Thrones are where kings sit, right? And, since Jesus sits at the right hand of the Father, and since we are seated with Christ in heavenly places—well, guess what: You are royalty!

Now, who would ever want to leave a place like that? Most of us would like to bring our sleeping bags and camp there a while. Take a moment and read Isaiah 6. Imagine observing the angels crying out, "Holy, holy, holy is the Lord Almighty." Witnessing this glory and the doorposts moving at His voice would cause us, like Isaiah, to be totally awestruck.

But, oh! My goodness, what about that angel with tongs and the hot coal? He touched it to Isaiah's lips—how painful that must have been. Was God punishing Isaiah? Had Isaiah "hung out" too long with an old king (a particular season or perhaps a stronghold)? No. God Himself was purifying Isaiah. I love how God's grace simply takes over any time we need help. The angel declared, "See, this coal has touched your lips. Now your guilt is removed, and your sins are forgiven" (Isaiah 6:7, NLT). Isaiah had to be cleansed from impure thoughts, sins and iniquity before he could approach the throne and be given strategies to proceed into his destiny. God, in His mercy and goodness, prepared him for the ministry ahead.

After Isaiah was cleansed, he heard the voice of the Lord saying, "'Whom shall I send? And who will go for us?' And [he] said, 'Here am I. Send me!'" (Isaiah 6:8). So the Lord sent him, complete with fresh strategies to move mountains and change governments.

So let's review. In order to receive direction for his life, Isaiah first had to move past the death of an old thing, to visit the Lord in His throne room, to witness His glory and to be cleansed from impure thoughts, sins and iniquity. Isaiah desired to be sent forth, but his sending only happened because the other steps had been accomplished first.

Are we willing to move past a season and serve the Lord in a fresh way? Or will we shut our mouths, roll up our sleeping gear and run for dear life? We cannot allow past guilt, disappointments, despair, fear or trauma to keep us from approaching the throne of God for a fresh touch and a fresh cleansing of Jesus' precious blood. Holiness comes from being righteous *in Christ*. Remind yourself of that daily. Say to yourself now,

I am righteous in Christ Jesus; therefore, He lives in me. I have prepared for Him a holy tabernacle. Today I am cleansed and holy and prepared for His service. I am royalty and I shall possess my full inheritance through Christ Jesus.

Isaiah was sent out from the throne room with God's power and authority. He knew who he was—he was God's messenger. This prophet had a fresh strategy, fresh empowerment and fresh direction after his throne room experience. Isaiah was "sent" from the throne room to reform political and social wrongs, to confront witches and soothsayers, to challenge the wealthy and to denounce ungodly kings. He also foretold the birth of the Messiah and gave specific prophetic instruction to the godly kings. Now, that is what I call heavenly strategy!

We are living in an apostolic age. The word *apostle* means "sent one." Like Isaiah, our authority in the spirit realm is given to us because we are sent out with authority.

There are some differences, however. The strategies Isaiah received were somewhat different from warfare strategies we might receive from the Lord today. Isaiah gave prophetic demonstrations, such as going barefoot for three years and wearing only a loincloth (see Isaiah 20:2–6). He was instructed to do this during a time in biblical history when society measured status by meticulous dress codes.

Today status is measured in similar ways, but a prophet who wore only a loincloth would most likely be arrested for indecent exposure! We must hear God's instruction for our time today, not times past, and in order to hear Him clearly, we, like Isaiah, must be positioned at His throne.

## A New Door Has Opened

The throne room awaits us. We are children of the King, and He bids us enter. It is in that place that we will learn to walk in the power of the blood and embrace our royal inheritance.

Are you ready to receive specific direction from the throne of God? The Lord is inviting you to come up to a new level, a new dimension, because He wants to help you move out of past difficulties and receive fresh strategies for a new season of life. His voice is as a trumpet sounding forth.

After this I looked, and there before me was a door standing open in heaven. And the voice I had first heard speaking to me like a trumpet said, "*Come up here*, and I will show you what must take place after this." At once I was in the Spirit, and there before me was *a throne in heaven* with someone sitting on it.

Revelation 4:1–2 (emphasis added)

# — 1 —

# DANCING WITH THE KING

> [We have,] therefore, brethren, boldness to enter into the holy
> place by the blood of Jesus.
>
> Hebrews 10:19, ASV

You are born to rule! Yes, this book is based on that truth
and will progressively reveal keys to empower you to possess your divine destiny. Dear one, the Holy Spirit is available
to you, right now, to lead and assist you in possessing your
*royal inheritance.*

Since the Fall in the Garden of Eden, mankind has had
an identity crisis. We know the story—how Satan deceived
Adam and Eve and stole their dominion on the earth. God,
however, had a backup plan to restore dominion to us. His
plans for our success in life have never been altered. His plan
of redemption was formed before the foundation of the world
(see Ephesians 1:4). From the beginning God had purposed
that a blood sacrifice would redeem mankind. How wonderful

it is to understand the importance of the cross: The blood of Jesus has reconciled us with the Father. Eternal life in His presence is now possible. Yes, God has *invested Himself* in you.

The book you hold in your hand is an investment of the Spirit of God to endow you with supernatural understanding regarding the power of the blood of Jesus and the blood covenant. My heart is to pray with you along your journey and help you understand how much He desires for you to achieve your royal inheritance. You are a child of the Most High. You have *royal blood* flowing through you.

### A Dream with *You* in It

The Lord visited me one night with a powerful dream that involves *you*. Yes, God cares so much about *you* that He gave me a dream to empower every reader of this book. This dream concerns *you* because in the dream I was commissioned to lead others to discover their destinies and connect them to their royal inheritance. You are that person, right now, whom the Holy Spirit is helping discover a royal inheritance and take possession of the prophetic promises. God has a promised land for you, and, now, the Spirit of God desires to lead *you* into its fullness.

The dream was specific about two things. First, I was commissioned to invest my time and energy into the Body of Christ as each person uncovers strongholds that hold him or her captive. Second, I am to help the Body discern and possess the blessings of royal inheritance.

Let's look briefly at the definition of a stronghold. Put simply, a *stronghold* is "anything that has a *strong hold* on us, anything that holds us captive or enslaves us." To quote Scripture, it is "every pretension that sets itself up against the knowledge of God" (2 Corinthians 10:5).

Observe that word *pretension*. Notice how closely it resembles the word *pretend*. Satan tries to pretend that he is God. He lies and attempts to make his voice sound like God's voice. He is seductive and cunning, and his goal is to destroy every destiny we have in Christ.

Strongholds get their grip on us because of sin—even if our sin comes in response to painful events like trauma, death, infirmity or lack. Satan uses these strongholds to gain entry into our lives, and then, like a squatter, maintains legal residence. What is more, since the pattern of sin—the stronghold—usually continues down the family line, he can stake his claim on succeeding generations.

It is vital to recognize any sin that has opened the door to Satan, seek God's forgiveness and be released from the stronghold. We must drive out any demonic squatters and reclaim what is legally ours, including the blessings that have been blocked sometimes for generations.

On this journey we will discover what strongholds have dwarfed God in our minds and hearts. We will examine any areas other than God Himself that have become a preoccupation. This means that we must understand our true identity, our righteousness in Christ and the power of the blood of Jesus.

Now, back to the dream!

## The Dream Begins

The setting for my dream was Westminster Abbey in London. I consider this a powerful symbol for us as believers because of its royal significance through the centuries. In my dream, I was joined by a ministry team on a spiritual search for mysteries that had been hidden from us, but that God was ready to reveal. These truths seemed "buried," much as the numerous monarchs are entombed at the Abbey. We were on our way to discover how God would reveal the hidden mysteries—regarding, specifically, our royal inheritance—"for such a time as this."

I was wheeling my carry-on luggage briskly through the airport trying to find our gate. Members of the team with me hurried along as well, and soon they began asking me the purpose of our trip. Actually, at that point I had no clue why we were traveling down that particular path. Still, they asked me over and over, "Why? Why? Why?" I was supposed to know the answer, but until I opened my mouth to speak I had no idea what that answer would be.

Suddenly words flew out of my mouth. "Well, the Lord told me to take a team to London, and actually I believe that it is to discover our inheritances. It has something to do with royal blood," I said. "Our inheritances have been hidden, as mysteries, and I am the leader in charge of a spiritual expedition to help us discover and claim them."

At that point I awoke briefly. I realized that I was in the midst of an important dream—one that was given for the Body of Christ. I became very excited and suddenly felt the presence of the Holy Spirit in my room. Then a "covering" fell upon my body. I know now that He was releasing a mantle of authority over me.

Silently, in my heart, I said, *Lord, please take me where I need to go to fulfill my destiny and empower others to claim their spiritual inheritance.* I fell back asleep and the dream continued.

## The Secret Chambers

Now that I had some idea of the purpose of our trip, I could ponder, as we hurried along, just what the Lord was doing. I knew that every believer has an incredible inheritance from the Lord, and that it is connected to our covenant blessing.

My responsibility was to disconnect the individuals with me from whatever had separated them from their inheritance—even through many generations. I was to reconnect them with the royal bloodline.

We finally found the proper gate and boarded the plane. As I looked around at the other passengers, I was honored to see that many respected leaders in the Body of Christ were on this same mission.

The scene changed. Now we were entering a secret chamber connected to Westminster Abbey. It was a narrow, hidden entrance—and before that moment, undiscovered. There are many passages in Scripture that describe how God has withheld revelation, keeping things *secret* for a specific time or season of release. (See Mark 4:11, AMP; Mark 4:22; Luke 8:17; Romans 16:25; and Colossians 2:2, to name just a few passages.)

Once within the chamber, we looked around to see the tombs of our past generations. Each tomb was covered by a "breastplate." The Old Testament teaches us that the priest wore a breastplate, but in this dream the breastplate was represented as a *weapon of warfare*. These breastplates displayed keys revealing how every generation of that family was to possess its royal inheritance. Ephesians 6:14 describes it as a *breastplate of righteousness*. It was also certain that this breastplate, which is connected to our righteousness in Christ, would empower us with greater understanding of the Kingdom of heaven and how to experience heaven on earth . . . *now*!

This is significant for you, dear one. The Lord was showing me that we must understand how to use this breastplate of righteousness to renew our minds. We must understand its significance and how it is connected to our royal inheritance. In fact, I am completely convinced that unless we understand that we are righteous *only* because of the righteousness of Christ, we will not be able to battle properly for our future.

I would like for you to focus on the breastplate as a "covering." The breastplate covered each tomb and generational royal inheritance, but it was also connected to the blood covenant—which we will discuss in the next chapter in detail.

Covering is a very important theme in Scripture. God "covered" or "mantled" Adam and Eve with His glory, and later through a blood sacrifice continued to cover mankind. (That means we, today, can be covered by the blood.)

On the negative side, when Satan deceived Eve, she covered herself with fig leaves—she was covered with "shame." Mankind has battled shame ever since. Since shame involves a lost sense of *right standing*, it is easy to see how the enemy uses it to oppose our gift of righteousness through Christ.

Over the years of battling a stronghold of shame—in my life and in others' lives—I have seen many rubble-strewn wastelands, including in the generations. It is God's desire to cause us to bloom—even while in the desert. Take a few moments and read Isaiah 35. This is your promise to hold on to while we travel down the road to full restoration.

Okay, back to the breastplate. Exodus describes the breastplate that the high priest wore, including twelve gemstones representing each of the twelve tribes of Israel. There is much controversy among biblical scholars about the different tribal gemstones. My focus is not on the stones, their colors, etc., except to recognize the significance of their beauty, the assignments of the tribes connected to the stones and the fact that each stone represented something special from God. Knowing that the twelve tribes were directed to go possess their Promised Land, I believe that my dream represented our royal inheritance to claim and possess our promises.

For those of us within the dream, the message became clear. The royal blood covers us and connects us to our royal and spiritual inheritance through Christ Jesus. There is power in the blood; now is the season for believers to uncover what has been hidden and seize what is rightfully ours. By discovering these hidden truths, we are becoming aligned with all that God says about us and wants to do through us.

The Lord desires to reveal everything that will help us be freed from captivity and reclaim what is rightfully ours. I kept thinking to myself during the dream, *I have an inheritance in Christ Jesus; I am here to receive my full portion! There is power in the blood of Jesus.*

## Fresh Revelation

Beloved, listen up a minute. God is breathing afresh upon His Word, and we must refrain from limiting God's truths with our mind-sets and doctrines. Much of what we believe is restricted by legalism. (We will discuss this in a later chapter.) The more revelation I receive from God, the more I realize that I have limited Him—especially whenever I examine Scriptures such as 1 Corinthians 1:30–31, which says:

> It is because of [God] that you are in Christ Jesus, who has become for us wisdom from God—that is, our righteousness, holiness and redemption. Therefore, as it is written: "Let him who boasts boast in the Lord."

Many of us have limited God when it comes to "righteousness" and "holiness." We do this every time we believe that it is all up to us and our own efforts to remain righteous. Take it from someone who has "been there and done that." If you and I depend on our own ability to be righteous and holy, we are going to develop a *works mentality*. (More on that later also!) I fell into this trap because I did not understand how to depend upon the power in the blood and how to claim my spiritual inheritance.

This is why we must remember that one of our spiritual weapons for warfare is the "breastplate of righteousness." We are protected as we war against the enemy because we stand in righteousness—*and this is possible only through the righteousness we have in Christ Jesus.* Righteousness cannot be earned by doing good works or praying long hours or even fasting. *Righteousness is a gift.* Our royal inheritance is also a gift. Think about this for a minute: You do not have to work for a gift. God has given us the free gift of righteousness, so stop trying to be righteous by working for it.

If we keep reminding ourselves that we are righteous through Christ Jesus and that we have been bought with the price of His blood, we will not walk in condemnation. It is so simple, but we make it complicated.

A King died for you and me. He was buried in a tomb. When He died, He made us sons and daughters; we are His inheritance. By grace we are saved, and through that grace we are no longer to be condemned. Sin no longer has power over us.

Now, that with that simple explanation, picture yourself at a grand ball, preparing to step onto the floor in perfect rhythm—in a dance with the King.

## Dancing with the King

At the end of the dream, we were all excited to be exploring the things that had been locked up for so long. We realized that we were ready to walk in our authority and receive our inheritance through Christ.

I was thrilled to begin helping each person prepare for something wonderful: We were going to enter a ballroom for a marvelous, majestic dance with the King. I can only tell you that the anticipation was electric. The thought of dancing with the King, being embraced by His power, was joyous beyond words.

It is that sense of excitement and splendor that I hope to share with you as you, too, prepare to "dance" with Jesus. To *dance* with Him in closeness and intimacy is a picture of how God always gives us access to His heart. We have been washed in the blood of the Lamb, cleansed and made righteous through Christ Jesus. We can always come boldly to His throne and receive forgiveness and grace. It is His desire to release His very best to each of us.

When we have messed up and feel ashamed, we usually run *from* Jesus rather than *to* Him. That is not His desire. He wants us to know that He never condemns—He just continues to love us.

Now, I do not advocate sinning just because we have already been forgiven. No way! The grace message has been misunderstood in the past. The definition of *grace* is not simply a divine empowerment from God to fulfill destiny; it is also undeserved favor. We should receive His gift of grace with humility. Remember, there is nothing we can do to earn our own righteousness. Knowing this will empower you to envision yourself dancing with your King.

But there is more.

## Dancing Is Intimacy

The word for "dancing," in both Greek and Hebrew, is associated with "intimacy" and "birthing." In Hebrew it is related to the word *chuwl* (pronounced "khool") or *chiyl* (pronounced "kheel"), a primitive root meaning "to twist or whirl, to dance, to writhe in pain." Look at some of the other words connected with dancing found in my reference dictionaries: "to bring forth, calve, fall in fear, be grievous, hope, look, rest, shake, shape, stay, tarry, tremble, trust and wait."

What does this aspect of dancing with the King have to do with "bringing forth" or "birthing"? It has to do with birthing our future. As you move in intimacy and closeness with Him, you will see that your future is pregnant with potential and possibilities. A royal inheritance awaits your possession. Much of this inheritance has been buried, hidden and locked away—just waiting for you to access it. As you discover how righteous you already are due to the blood of Jesus and how much power is available through that blood, you will begin to walk in your true identity as a child of the King.

Birthing involves the travail of pressing through a restricted, narrow place; natural birthing always involves passing through the birth canal. Perhaps even now you are passing through a narrow place, being pressed in by the enemy, as you move toward your promises. Listen carefully as we journey together. Grab a pen or pencil and take notes. God will speak . . . will you listen?

### Following His Lead

Before you turn the page, ask yourself these questions:

1. Do I fully understand that I am royalty?
2. Am I ready to comprehend what my inheritance is and to apprehend it?
3. Am I ready to come out of a wilderness mentality and allow the Spirit of God to challenge my doctrines and belief systems that attempt to hold me captive?
4. Am I ready to receive a new mantle of authority that empowers me to possess my future?
5. Do I fully grasp the truths concerning the power that is in the blood of Jesus?
6. Am I walking in my God-given authority and blessings?

7. Do I truly believe that I am a "King's kid" and a son or daughter of God who has a destiny that involves being fruitful and multiplying?
8. Do I desire to see myself with the eyes of heaven and agree with God concerning His will for my life?
9. Do I understand that God desires to release the culture of heaven to earth?
10. Can I picture myself as an active soldier in God's army called by Him to pray and bring heaven to earth?
11. Will I allow the Holy Spirit to examine my heart as He also empowers me to fulfill my destiny? His Word says that there is hope for me (see Jeremiah 29:11). Can I seize it today?
12. Do I realize that I am holy and righteous—but *only* because of the blood?

Now let me ask you one more question: Are you ready to meet Jesus face to face? When you dance with the King, you are going to see Him as He is. What a glorious time awaits you as you determine in your heart to know more about Him and His plans for your future.

If you are a new believer, some of these questions might seem overwhelming. Perhaps you have faced hopeless situations because you did not understand the power of the blood of Jesus and how He desires for you to lay claim to your inheritance. You may fear meeting God face to face. Let me assure you that there is nothing to fear. This simply means that He desires more intimacy with you. God desires to draw each of us nearer to Him. Trust Him—He is leading you to a glorious future.

Jesus is waiting to dance with you, to release His inheritance to you. Come with me. The King is calling us. Let's discover our glorious inheritance together.

# — 2 —

# THE BLOOD AND THE
# ATONEMENT

Not only is this so, but we also rejoice in God through our
Lord Jesus Christ, through whom we have now received
reconciliation.

Romans 5:11

*The power of the blood of Jesus.*
Everything we need to know about possessing all that
God has promised us is summed up in those few words. Our
power to reign in life and claim our spiritual inheritance rests
entirely on Jesus Christ and His shed blood.

Romans 5:17 helps us begin to build on this foundation:

For if, by the trespass of the one man, death reigned through
that one man, how much more will those who receive God's

abundant provision of grace and of *the gift of righteousness reign in life* through the one man, Jesus Christ.

(emphasis added)

The word *reign* in this particular passage is the Greek word *basileuo* (pronounced bas-il-*yoo*-o), which *Strong's* concordance tells us refers to ruling or reigning as a king. If you recall my dream in the last chapter, I was preparing the saints to dance with the King. We were also on a spiritual quest to possess our inheritance. We were uncovering mysteries that were connected to "royalty." Well, how obvious can it be! A king is royal, right? It is safe to conclude, therefore, that because of the gift of righteousness Christ gave us through the shedding of His royal blood, we are also royalty and are empowered to rule and reign.

And there is more. *Unger's* dictionary describes *basileuo* as "the reign of God through the entrance of Christ." This means that we have the power of God within us because Jesus entered the world as a man and gave His life as a perfect sacrifice so that we could be empowered from heaven with godly dominion and authority.

This book is about exalting Jesus Christ because He willingly went to the cross and took our sins upon Himself. Yes, He became sin and suffered death so that we would never have to face eternal punishment. Now, we all must lay "self" on the altar—we must die to self—if we desire to enthrone Jesus in our hearts, but because of Jesus' sacrifice we never have to experience eternal separation from God.

In this chapter we will look more closely into Jesus' sacrifice and how we were reconciled to God through it. Until we understand this act, known as the atonement, we will never appreciate what Christ has done for us. And until we understand our need for a savior, we will never comprehend the bondage of our sin.

Let's begin there.

## The Offense of Sin

Most of us have some idea of what sin is. Sin is the basic problem of humanity, for all ages. It is also a problem for us individually, whether we have recognized it or not. We are all born with a sin nature. Romans 3:23 states this clearly: "All have sinned and fall short of the glory of God." When we sin, we fall short of God's glory. That alone makes me not want to sin. How about you?

In Hebrew, *sin* is the word *chatta'ah* (pronounced khat-taw-*aw*) or *chatta'th* (khat-*tawth*), and it means "offense." Throughout the Bible we learn that sin offends God, and that sin is a punishable offense by a righteous and holy God.

According to Old Testament Law, covenant sacrifices—the blood of animals—were necessary to reconcile sinful mankind to God. We read in Hebrews 9:22 that "under the Law almost everything is purified by means of blood, and without the shedding of blood there is neither release from sin and its guilt nor the remission of the due and merited punishment for sins" (AMPLIFIED). Thus, we read in the Old Testament how God's people dealt with sin by offering a blood sacrifice to the Lord. That offering covered mankind and atoned for the penalties of sin.

In Hebrew, the word for *atonement* is *kippur* (pronounced kip-*poor*) and it means "covering." The Day of Atonement—*Yom Kippur*—began as an annual ceremonial day of "covering," when sacrifices for the people's sins were offered to God. By this act on that one day, the sins of Israel were forgiven—but only for one year. The same ceremony was required a year later. The Day of Atonement, which is still observed but without animal sacrifices, is no permanent solution for the sins of the people; it is merely a temporary covering.

In the New Testament the concept of sin takes on a different shade of meaning. *Sin* in Greek is *hamartano* (pronounced ham-ar-*tan*-o) and it means "to miss the mark and so not share in the prize." It also means "to err," connecting it particularly to moral sin.

Sin offends God, and when we sin, we also fall short of the prize. Sin is not always committing a terrible crime; it is also about not giving God first place in our lives. In other words—*He is the prize we seek!* Sin is all about failing to give God His rightful place in our hearts and lives. When we live in sin, we are not giving God the glory He deserves, and we are withheld from receiving His glory.

Thank God we have a remedy! The Bible, the inerrant Word of God, diagnoses our sin and offers the final and complete remedy: the cross. If we desire to possess our full spiritual inheritance, we must focus on the finished work at the cross through the shedding of Jesus' precious blood.

The book of Hebrews describes most vividly Jesus as our High Priest and the sacrifice He made on our behalf. First, Hebrews 10:4 explains that the Old Testament sacrificial system was not a conclusive solution: "It is impossible for the blood of bulls and goats to take away sins." The central issue lies in the "taking away" of sins and not merely "covering them."

Hebrews 9:26 shows that Jesus' sacrifice was that perfect plan: "[Christ] appeared once for all . . . to do away with sin by the sacrifice of himself." Two other passages in the book of Hebrews contrast Jesus' act with the Old Testament priesthood, explaining that He became the *ultimate sacrifice and offering*:

> Such a high priest meets our need—one who is holy, blameless, pure, set apart from sinners, exalted above the heavens. Unlike the other high priests, he does not need to offer sacrifices day after day, first for his own sins, and then for the sins of

the people. He sacrificed for their sins *once for all when he offered himself.*

Hebrews 7:26–27 (emphasis added)

Look at the word *offer* for a moment. *Offer* refers to the action of priests when they make a sacrifice for sin. *Jesus offered Himself on the cross as the final offering for all sin.* Jesus, as High Priest, offered the sacrifice, but He, Himself, as Lamb, also became the ultimate sacrifice for our sin. This offering paid the price forever for our victory—and allows us to claim our spiritual inheritance.

The other passage in Hebrews further explains this contrast:

The blood of goats and bulls and the ashes of a heifer sprinkled on those who are ceremonially unclean sanctify them so that they are outwardly clean. How much more, then, will *the blood of Christ, who through the eternal Spirit offered himself unblemished to God,* cleanse our consciences from acts that lead to death, so that we may serve the living God!

Hebrews 9:13–14 (emphasis added)

This is the Good News, the Gospel message: *Jesus has put away sin by the sacrifice of Himself.* When John the Baptist saw Jesus, the Sacrifice, approaching to receive baptism, he said, "Behold, the lamb of God who *takes away* the sin of the world." Jesus took away the need for further sacrifice for sins.

That is worth jumping up and down about! No longer do we have to dash out to the barnyard and grab a spotless lamb and then slaughter it. Oh, that would be so hard for me because I love those woolly creatures! And, then, we would have to repeat the same thing at the same time the next year.

Jesus' one-time, perfect sacrifice has reconciled us to God. Believer, take a moment and ponder the following passage: "Since that time he waits for his enemies to be made his footstool, because by one sacrifice he has made perfect forever those who are being made holy" (Hebrews 10:13–14).

The shedding of Jesus' blood completed the needed sacrifice for sin—forever! When He took on Himself the punishment we sinners deserve, He atoned for, or paid the penalty for, all sin for all time. This means that when we confess our sins with repentant hearts, Jesus' work of atonement connects us to God and opens the way for us to spend eternity with Him, and to possess our royal inheritance now.

We have a wonderful reminder within the word *atonement* itself of what Jesus accomplished for us if we divide the syllables a certain way—like this: *at-one-ment*. The atonement gives every individual the opportunity to become one with Him (see Galatians 3:28).

If only we could wrap our hearts and minds around this truth—that God is not mad at us when we sin, and that He is not going to punish us simply because He is offended. No! What happens is this: Sin separates us from God. It causes us to miss out on achieving our full potential. We miss the mark and are not able to share in the good things He desires for us—not only eternity in His presence but also the inheritance that we can enjoy on this earth. The Lord longs for us to reach our potential and claim our spiritual inheritances. *He is never mad at us. He desires to empower us to win the prize through His grace.* That is why He wants us to repent of our sins and accept the gift of salvation.

In the simplest words, *repentance* means "changing our minds." For years I thought that shame was a prerequisite to repentance, but it is not. Nor does God desire to punish us before we repent. When we repent we realize that we have gone beyond a godly boundary and missed out on God's best. We then change our minds concerning our directions and our actions.

## The Offering

There is no way that we could possess all the good God has for us except for the blood of Jesus being shed at the cross. Too often we, as believers, receive the promise of something good, like healing, and apply our faith to achieve the potential within that word, but we ignore what Jesus did to empower us with the victory to possess the promise within that word! Dear one, to claim your spiritual inheritance, you must also consider the blood and continually "apply" the blood over your promises. (More on that later.)

Once we understand that Jesus (through His eternal Spirit) offered Himself without spot to God, we more fully understand this incredible sacrifice. First, He had to live a sinless life on earth as a mortal man. He overcame sin and all temptation connected to sin, and as the spotless Lamb became an offering for our sins. Second, at the cross He became the Priest and the victim. Third, He was completely pure and His blood was pure. As the Son of God, He was of royal blood. Because we are one in Christ, we have the blood of Jesus in our own veins. Oh, are you forever thankful for the blood of Jesus?

I love the thought that I am righteous through Christ's righteousness. Again, this means that I do not have to perform for God to be righteous. Let's look at Romans 5:17 once more—notice that righteousness is a *gift*:

> For if, by the trespass of the one man, death reigned through that one man, how much more will those who receive God's abundant provision of grace and of *the gift of righteousness* reign in life through the one man, Jesus Christ.
>
> (emphasis added)

God's way for us to be successful in life is simply to receive. His way is about receiving rather than achieving. Believers, I know this revelation is setting you free. The way to reign as royalty is to receive His righteousness.

For years I believed that I had to work at being holy. I was bent on doing . . . doing . . . doing. I never understood the simplicity of receiving. I believed that if I studied the Word, could quote the Word and stand on the Word that I would then be holy. That becomes legalism! It is not a matter of how often we attend church or how long we pray. Our righteousness and holiness lie in the finished work of Christ and the shedding of His blood.

As you continue to read this book, see yourself as righteous and holy through the finished work of Christ. Take a look at where we are seated in the heavens as you reread Ephesians 2:4–6 (KJV):

> But God, who is rich in mercy, for his great love wherewith he loved us, even when we were dead in sins, hath quickened us together with Christ, (by grace ye are saved;) and hath raised us up together, and made us *sit together* in heavenly places in Christ Jesus.
>
> (emphasis added)

Yes, we can actually "sit down," knowing that we are seated together with Christ and His finished work at the cross.

I am positive that as you continue to read, you will gain knowledge of heaven's strategies to defeat the enemy and claim your inheritance. God is promising you victory. Your faith is growing and all condemnation is leaving. You have realized that as you dance with the King, you are also endowed with power from heaven. You are righteous because of the blood. There is no more condemnation—you have been released from all of the shame of your past!

Now, read on. More freedom awaits you as you gain even more strategy to rule and reign through the blood of Christ.

# — 3 —

# THE BLOOD COVENANT
# AND OUR INHERITANCE

An inheritance, put simply, is a gift of earthly wealth or possessions given at the time of the death of the owner. Inheritance is a primary focus in Scripture, as the children of Israel gave a great deal of attention to either obtaining possession or keeping possession of their Promised Land, granted them by God through their patriarch Abraham.

As children of Abraham by faith, inheritance is equally important to all believers. I am not speaking here of the land of Israel, the inheritance of the Jewish people, but rather the spiritual inheritance God has granted us through Jesus Christ.

What is this inheritance? To find out, we begin at the beginning. Let's turn to what is termed "first mention" in the Bible of the word *inheritance*. The first time something is spoken of in the Bible is always significant. When God called Abraham out of Ur of the Chaldees, He gave Abraham this promise: "And He said to him, I am the [same] Lord, Who brought you out of Ur of the Chaldees to give you this land as an inheritance"(Genesis 15:7, AMPLIFIED).

In this passage the inheritance is land that Abraham's descendants would occupy and take possession of. In other words, God told Abraham that his inheritance to future generations was a "Promised Land," and that it would be Abraham's seed who would fulfill the promise by driving out the inhabitants and occupying the territory. His children and generations to follow were to be blessed with land and prosperity.

To affirm this promise, God later changed the name of Abraham's grandson from *Jacob* to *Israel*. The name *Israel* means "prince of God." Here we can see the testimony of a royal inheritance. God identifies Himself as the God of Israel—God over an entire nation of royal princes.

Now, this is a word of promise that has an added dimension. It is true not only for Abraham's *physical* descendants, the Jewish people, but also for his *spiritual* descendants. Galatians 3:29 says that "if ye are Christ's, then are ye Abraham's seed, heirs according to promise" (ASV). This means that those who believe in Jesus receive the blessings of Abraham. And also, according to Romans 8:17, we are joint heirs, or co-heirs, with Christ, meaning that we share in His sufferings but also in His glory. According to 1 Peter 3:7, because we are joint heirs with Christ we are able to share in the *grace of life*, or the *gracious gift of life*.

For two thousand years, from the time of Abraham to Jesus, God purposefully prepared a people to know and understand how to possess and walk in His covenant blessings. This inheritance is meant for us as believers to share as well. We can claim our incredible inheritance now! We can walk in this unmerited favor today.

Jacob (later named Israel) had twelve sons who became heads of the twelve tribes of Israel. We discuss this in a later chapter, but for now know that each tribe had an inheritance (a Promised Land) to possess. Each tribe possessed a redemptive destiny, which is an example for us today, as we also have a destiny to claim and possess.

As I stated in the introduction, it was the Issachar tribe that understood the times and seasons of God. Believer, let me assure you that it is our season to walk in blessings and freedom. The problem with many of us is that our identities in Christ have been submerged in hopelessness, despair, shame and discouragement. Our freedom in Christ has been dormant due to our believing lies about ourselves. We have believed the lie that we are unworthy and, therefore, do not deserve to be blessed. When we realize that we are already "righteous" because of the blood of Jesus, we can begin to rise up and take our rightful position.

Let me assure you of this one thing: Satan hates the mention of the blood of Jesus. I have witnessed bondages break off of people when we mention the blood. Demons have to flee when we talk about the blood of Jesus. When Christ was crucified, His shed blood redeemed us from sin and death. Yes! He overcame death, hell and the grave. The Holy Spirit then came to teach us all things, and to comfort and direct us.

This proves that there is no favor from God apart from the blood covenant that He has instituted. Without the blood there is no grace, blessing, power, reconciliation or fellowship with God. Without the blood, God is basically absent from our lives! It is only through the blood of Jesus that we can walk with and have restored fellowship with God. It is through the blood that we receive our inheritance.

### The Firstborn Inheritance Is Ours

In the Old Testament, we read that whenever the father of a Hebrew household died, the firstborn son became the anointed priest of that particular family. The authority of the father was passed to the firstborn son. This son was the one chosen to receive the "double portion inheritance."

We are all, according to Scripture, God's firstborn sons. We have obtained the status of being not only priests but also kings. Observe Revelation 5:10 and keep in mind that God called Israel His firstborn son: "And hast made us unto our God kings and priests: and we shall reign on the earth" (KJV). Since the Church is God's "spiritual Israel," we receive the firstborn inheritance, which includes power and dominion over all of the power of the enemy as well as our covenant blessings.

We are destined to *rise up*! During the Old Testament period, the Church was a "mystery"—a secret kept hidden throughout the generations. We see these mysteries revealed in the New Testament to the apostles and prophets (see Ephesians 3:3–9; Colossians 1:25–27). As you recall, God showed me through my dream that I was given the privilege to empower many people to uncover hidden mysteries that blocked them from receiving their royal inheritance through Christ. This book is the fulfillment of that dream—we are uncovering mysteries that have held us captive and ill equipped to possess our promises.

Psalm 149 mentions singing a new song to the Lord and says to "praise His name with dancing." I love this passage, especially since it is referring to our dancing with the King. This *new* song translates as something not only "fresh" but also "repaired." I want you to embrace the fact that many of us are being "repaired" by the hand of God. He is healing wounds and repairing the breaches in our lives. Isaiah 54 paints the most beautiful picture of how we actually sing over the barren and unfruitful places in our lives and see life come forth.

Psalm 149 goes on to say that when we praise God and dance, we break the chains of our captivity and the clutches of the enemy. Get excited as you read this passage:

Praise the LORD.

Sing to the LORD a new song,
his praise in the assembly of the saints.

Let Israel rejoice in their Maker;
let the people of Zion be glad in their King.
Let them praise his name with dancing
and make music to him with tambourine and harp.
For the LORD takes delight in his people;
he crowns the humble with salvation.
Let the saints rejoice in this honor
and sing for joy on their beds.

May the praise of God be in their mouths
and a double-edged sword in their hands,
to inflict vengeance on the nations
and punishment on the peoples,
to bind their kings with fetters,
their nobles with shackles of iron,
to carry out the sentence written against them.
This is the glory of all his saints.

Praise the LORD.

Psalm 149

Old Testament prophecies, when rightly discerned and understood, tell us much about the period of the restoration of the Church and how we today can claim our promised inheritances. Do you recall the prophecy given to Ezekiel when he was in the valley of dry bones? Grab your Bible and read Ezekiel 37:1–10 and refresh your memory as to how the Spirit of the Lord came upon him in a vision and told Ezekiel to prophesy to the dry bones.

In the beginning of the vision, God's children are pictured as dry, disjointed and scattered bones, but when the Spirit of God supernaturally moves upon those dry bones, they come together and are connected by "joints." Then muscles, ligaments, flesh and skin cover the joints and bones. Next, God breathes upon these bones and they rise up and become an "exceedingly great army."

I like talking about "joints" when I preach, because in Ephesians 4:16 (KJV) Paul says that God's purpose for us is that we, as a body, are knit and held together by every supporting joint. But I also like to apply it to our being *joint heirs* with Christ. I am joined together with Him and, therefore, receive my full inheritance. He is the Head of all things and we are His Body—fitly joined together; therefore, we are one in Christ.

I picture the ligaments that came upon the bones as covenant, because in the natural body, the ligaments are bands of tissue that hold bones together at the place where they are joined. What connects us firmly to our promises and our inheritance is the covenant of God. When we understand that that covenant makes us joint heirs we can then lay claim to our future.

Now, let's look at how the blood covenant was instituted and reenacted at key times in biblical history. The power in the blood of the Lamb awaits your claim!

## The Blood Covenant Is Established

When God created man, he was perfect because he was created in the image and likeness of God. Also, man had perfect fellowship with God. But when sin came into the heart of Eve through the deception of the enemy, Adam entered into sin with her and they became separated from God. Their fellowship with God was broken because of their sin. Yet, God came looking for them—knowing they had sinned. Dear one,

46

God will always seek after us—He never quits! I love the fact that God will *never not* pursue us.

### Adam and Eve Are Clothed

We all know this story, but let's revisit what happened in the Garden to fully understand the beginning and purpose of the blood covenant. After they had sinned, Adam and Eve were ashamed and covered themselves with fig leaves. They had previously been clothed (covered) with God's glory, but after they sinned they lost that glory and realized their nakedness. Actually it was now shame that covered them. Because they were accustomed to being clothed they found fig leaves and covered themselves.

God came to them with a promise of redemption. The name *Jehovah God* is the blessed name of "God Almighty" or "the all-existing One," who is the God of covenant. The name *Elohim* is the God of creation, but *Jehovah* is the name that deals with His covenant. In other words, regarding Creation, we read about God as *Elohim*. Yet, regarding God as our covenant God, we read about *Jehovah*, the Lord God (or *Yahweh*). This is the name that represents His relationship with mankind.

So, even though mankind had sinned and rejected God, the Lord God sought after them and clothed them. In clothing them with coats of skins of animals, He was making a promise to redeem them. The Lord was actually expressing to Adam and Eve that they had an inappropriate covering. They could not cover themselves. No, only the Lord could cover them. It is the same for us today. We cannot cover ourselves. Only He can properly do this.

The word *cover* means "reconciliation." God came and covered them—to reconcile them to Himself. (We could also consider this as being "repaired" in one's relationship with the Lord.) Animals were slain to provide the coats. Thus, God performed the first sacrifice—which involved blood—to cover mankind. Imagine Him bringing coats to them—still stained with blood—and placing the coats upon their nakedness.

Blood was required to cover, and it is the same today. Blood is required to take away our sins and cover us with God's glory. In this covering of Adam and Eve, God was essentially saying, "I am purchasing mankind back." He was expressing to mankind that "I will do this." From that point forward, mankind could know God only through the shedding of blood.

### Cain and Abel Make Offerings

Adam taught his children about the blood sacrifice, as we read in Hebrews 11, which says that Abel, a son of Adam, "by faith" brought God an acceptable sacrifice. By observing what is written in Genesis 4, we see that Eve conceived once, but bore twice; therefore, Cain and Abel were twins. Of the two, it was Abel who honored the covenant process. Abel brought an offering of blood, the firstborn of his sheep, and Cain brought the fruit of the ground because he was a farmer, a tiller of the ground (see Genesis 4:3). Because God had established covenant and reconciliation through a blood sacrifice, Cain's offering was not acceptable. By faith, Abel brought the proper sacrifice.

God Almighty reckoned Abel as righteous, just as He had Abraham. Abel was righteous in God's eyes because of his faith to offer a more excellent sacrifice. And though he is dead today, this sacrifice still speaks—meaning that the blood covenant still stands.

### Noah Baptizes the Earth

Here is another story that all of us who were raised in church learned in Sunday school, a crucial story in the history of God's covenant with mankind. I can remember singing the song about Noah and the ark, and how all the animals came in two by two—but we were taught incorrectly! The clean animals were taken in by *sevens* and the unclean by *twos*. Let's look at Genesis 7:1–2:

> And the LORD said unto Noah, Come thou and all thy house into the ark; for thee have I seen righteous before me in this generation. Of every *clean beast thou shalt take to thee by sevens*, the male and his female: and of beasts that are *not clean by two*, the male and his female.
>
> KJV (emphasis added)

Go ahead, get your Bible out and read it again for yourself. Maybe you should highlight it in your Bible in case you hear someone question this fact. Do you know why God had the clean animals taken by sevens rather than twos? It was because the clean animals were needed for sacrifice. God did not accept any unclean animals. Only the clean animals could be an acceptable sacrifice as only "spotless" animals were acceptable later.

After Noah came out of the ark, Genesis 8:20 states that he built an altar to the Lord immediately and took one out of every seven clean animals to sacrifice as burnt offerings. Actually, Noah baptized the earth with blood—displaying covenant so that he could fellowship with God.

The blood covenant was the first thing he tended to when he left the ark. Imagine after forty days in the ark and another 120 days for the flood waters to settle, how that ark must have smelled. He was with those clean and unclean animals for quite a while, and yet those animals were first on his mind upon leaving the ark. Actually it was the Lord who was on his mind.

God smelled the sweet savor of the burnt offering and made a covenant, saying that He would never again curse the whole world with a flood. He set a rainbow in the sky as a sign of covenant—all because of the blood sacrifice. *The blood stopped the curse!* This is another reason the enemy hates the blood of Jesus: When we understand and appropriate the blood, we cannot be cursed. Whenever in deliverance sessions I recognize a generational curse upon someone's life, I break it off of the individual, reminding Satan that we cannot be cursed due to the shed blood of Jesus.

I love the following verse because it describes our royalty and the fact that the blood releases us from any curse of iniquity. Those of us of royal blood (we sons of God) cannot be cursed; we have the shout of a king within us.

> He has not observed misfortune in Jacob;
> Nor has He seen trouble in Israel;
> The LORD his God is with him,
> And the shout of a king is among them.
>
> Numbers 23:21, NASB

Dear one, the enemy will always attempt to cross bloodlines and find someone in the generations to whom he can attach a curse of disease, death or destruction. When we remind the devil that we are "blood bought," and that we have the shout of a king within us, we can break off every curse or evil assignment—generational or otherwise—and know we have victory. The sad thing is this: Many do not understand the authority we have in our blood covenant and never witness victory over curses or iniquity. This is the important message of this book: God desires that you understand who you are in Christ—victorious and blood bought!

### The Abrahamic Covenant Established

Abraham, after sojourning in Egypt and entering his place of promise, first made a sacrifice of blood (see Genesis 13:4).

Why was that the first thing he did? Well, like Noah, he desired fellowship with God. He made a blood sacrifice and called upon the name of the Lord. Take some time and read the entire chapter of Genesis 17, which describes in detail the covenant God made with Abraham. It is important to understand the *Abrahamic covenant* because, as we have determined, all believers are the spiritual seed of Abraham and can claim the same blessings.

Consider Abraham: "He believed God, and it was credited to him as righteousness" (Galatians 3:6). Those who believe in God are children of Abraham. The Scripture foresaw that God would justify the Gentiles by faith and announced the gospel in advance to Abraham (see Galatians 3:6–9): "All nations will be blessed through you" (verse 8). Those who have faith are blessed along with Abraham, the man of faith.

### Isaac Honors the Covenant

Abraham taught his son Isaac about the blood covenant. Genesis 26 states that when there was famine in the land, God instructed Isaac not to go to Egypt for provision. (Unlike what Abraham had done by going to Egypt!) During the famine, God gave Isaac specific instructions and promised to be in covenant with him as He had been with his father, Abraham:

> Dwell temporarily in this land, and I will be with you and will favor you with blessings; for to you and to your descendants I will give all these lands, and I will perform the oath which I swore to Abraham your father. And I will make your descendants to multiply as the stars of the heavens, and will give to your posterity all these lands (kingdoms); and by your Offspring shall all the nations of the earth be blessed, or by Him bless themselves.
>
> Genesis 26:3–4, AMPLIFIED

So Isaac stayed in Gerar, but it is interesting to note that he made the same error in judgment concerning his wife, Rebekah, that Abraham had made concerning Sarah! The men in Gerar started asking about Rebekah because of her beauty. Isaac was fearful that they would kill him in order to take her, so he lied (as his father had done while in Egypt) and told them she was his sister (see Genesis 26:7–11). God protected Rebekah, by letting the truth be known.

Isaac stayed in the land where God instructed, sowed seed into the ground and reaped a hundred-fold harvest. He became so wealthy that the Philistines in the land envied him. Now that is covenant blessing! Let's read about this in Genesis 26:

> Then Isaac sowed seed in that land and received in the same year a *hundred times* as much as he had planted, and the Lord favored him with blessings.
>
> And the man became great and gained more and more until he became very *wealthy* and *distinguished*; he owned flocks, herds, and a great supply of servants, and the Philistines envied him. . . .
>
> Now he went up from there to Beersheba. And the Lord appeared to him the same night and said, I am the God of Abraham your father. Fear not, for I am with you and will favor you with blessings and multiply your descendants for the sake of My servant Abraham.
>
> And [Isaac] *built an altar* there and called on the name of the Lord and pitched his tent there; and there Isaac's servants were digging a well.
>
> Genesis 26:12–14, 23–25, AMPLIFIED (emphasis added)

Notice that upon entering Beersheba (which means "well of the oath"), Isaac immediately build an altar and called upon the name of the Lord. Building an altar for blood sacrifice was the first thing he did. Once again, the land was baptized with blood so that he could continue to fellowship with God.

Let's review a minute. Adam, Abel, Noah, Abraham and Isaac all understood the blood covenant. Cain, however, did not understand it, and neither did Ishmael (Abraham's son by Hagar). Only the righteous understood blood covenant.

## Jacob Builds an Altar

Moving on, we study about Jacob, the son of Isaac. If you recall, he stole the birthright from his brother, Esau. He fled for his life knowing that Esau would seek to kill him. Much happened in Jacob's life after that, but 21 years later, Jacob returned home and faced Esau. The story is told in Genesis 33. Jacob purchased a field for one hundred pieces of silver and there he erected an altar unto the Lord.

> After Jacob came from Paddan Aram, he arrived safely at the city of Shechem in Canaan and camped within sight of the city. For a hundred pieces of silver, he bought from the sons of Hamor, the father of Shechem, the plot of ground where he pitched his tent. There he *set up an altar* and called it El Elohe Israel.
>
> Genesis 33:18–20 (emphasis added)

Once more we see there was much emphasis on the blood. God had revealed blood covenant to Adam, Abel, Noah, Abraham, Isaac and Jacob. These patriarchs understood the revelation behind the blood. Years and generations later (actually 430 years), the people of Israel had no fellowship with God. Their fathers mentioned Abraham and told stories of their history, but the Israelites in Egypt—now slaves—no longer worshiped God.

## Moses and the Passover

After centuries had passed, God called upon Moses to deliver Israel out of their bondage and lead them to the Promised

Land. Moses knew that the people would not listen to him—after all, following so many years of bondage, their hearts had hardened. God reestablished the blood covenant when He directed the Israelites to place lamb's blood upon the sides and tops of the doorframes of their homes. (This was a foreshadowing of Jesus' blood upon the doorposts of our hearts.)

More than three million Israelites took part in the Exodus (some theologians say two million; some suggest two million men plus wives and children) and, therefore, millions of lambs had to be sacrificed to protect them from the spirit of death, the final plague, that was sent to destroy Egypt's firstborn—of both men and animals. One lamb was sacrificed for each household—now that is a lot of lambs being sacrificed.

If you recall, there were ten plagues that God sent against Egypt. Every plague confronted an idol of Egypt. The first plague, for example, was directed toward the Egyptians' false gods *Hapi* and *Khenmu* (also known as *Khnum*). These were gods of the Nile. Ancient Egypt considered the Nile River to be their source of life. When the Nile flooded it deposited layers of fertile silt, making their crops flourish. Because Egypt worshiped these false gods as their provider rather than the Lord God, the plagues started there. If you recall, the Nile River was turned to blood.

The second plague was a plague of frogs, which was closely related to the first plague since the frogs came from the Nile River. Frogs were expected after the flood seasons, so the appearance of frogs was not unusual. God, however, sent a super abundance of frogs! Frogs were everywhere—the people could not walk without stepping on a frog. The false goddess associated with frogs was *Heket*. Chuck Pierce, in his insightful book *Time to Defeat the Devil* (Charisma, 2011), states:

> The goddess associated with frogs was *Heket*. She was a goddess of childbirth, creation and grain germination. As water

goddess, she was also a goddess of fertility and childbirth, particularly associated with the later stages of labor. . . . The Egyptians believed she gave a child the breath of life before it was placed in the mother's womb.

This, of course, defies *Elohim*, our Creator, and the One who told Jeremiah, "Before you were in your mother's womb I knew you."

The eight other plagues are named in Exodus 8, and they all oppose an Egyptian god. We will not discuss them in this book, but the topic is worthy of study. Take some time to understand the significance of the plagues.

Every plague sent was to put pressure on Pharaoh to "let God's people go." The first nine plagues caused Pharaoh's heart to be more hardened; he had no intention of releasing God's children from their bondage to Egypt. In the last plague, God confronted one of the highest false gods: *Pharaoh himself!* Yes! Pharaoh was considered to be a god. Not only was he the highest authority in Egypt, but also he demanded the people's worship. The plague of death for every firstborn in Egypt was directed at Pharaoh's firstborn son. Chuck Pierce writes:

In Exodus 4:22–23, God assured Moses that this plague would bring release for the people. This plague was the most serious of all because it involved the death of the firstborn. . . . This plague seemed terribly harsh, but we need to see that it was really Egypt's own sin revisited upon them. As Egypt had murdered the children of the Israelites and thrown the newborns into the Nile, so the just punishment that God inflicted on Egypt was that their own children would be forfeited.

It is important to understand that not every firstborn of Egypt had to die. The Egyptians could have chosen to renounce their false gods and join the Israelites in applying a lamb's blood to their doorframes. In fact, many of them possibly did this, as they might have been part of the group that left Egypt with the Israelites.

During the tenth plague, the firstborns of man and cattle all died—except in those homes covered by the blood and where the death angel passed over. (Read about this in Exodus 12.) This event became known as Passover and the Israelites have celebrated the blood covenant of Passover even to this day.

What a testimony once more of the blood covenant! God had proven His faithfulness by protecting those who had anointed their doorposts. Israel understood that the blood had protected them, keeping them and their descendants alive.

### The Wilderness Wanderings

After the Israelites were released from Egypt, the Lord led them into the desert to test their hearts. God still desired fellowship with His people. Again, He is *never not* pursuing us.

Let's read how the blood covenant between God and His people was confirmed while they were in the wilderness:

God said to Moses, Come up to the Lord, you and Aaron, Nadab and Abihu [Aaron's sons], and seventy of Israel's elders, and worship at a distance.

Moses alone shall come near the Lord; the others shall not come near, and neither shall the people come up with him.

Moses came and told the people all that the Lord had said and all the ordinances; and all the people answered with one voice, All that the Lord has spoken we will do.

Moses wrote all the words of the Lord. He rose up early in the morning and built an altar at the foot of the mountain and set up twelve pillars representing Israel's twelve tribes.

And he sent young Israelite men, who offered burnt offerings and sacrificed peace offerings of oxen to the Lord.

And Moses took half of the blood and put it in basins, and half of the blood he dashed against the altar.

Then he took the Book of the Covenant and read in the hearing of the people; and they said, All that the Lord has said we will do, and we will be obedient.

And Moses took the [remaining half of the] blood and sprinkled it on the people, and said, Behold the blood of the covenant which the Lord has made with you in accordance with all these words.

Exodus 24:1–8, AMPLIFIED
(see also 1 Corinthians 11:25; Hebrews 8:6; 10:28–29)

Did you notice that Moses took half of the blood of thousands of animals and put it in basins? He then sprinkled the remaining blood upon the altar and upon the people. Hebrews 9:19 states that Moses also sprinkled blood upon the Book of the Law.

Can you even imagine the sight of all of that blood—especially over three million people? Blood was everywhere! Thus, as the people stood before the Lord, He saw them *through the blood*. It is the same for us today: God sees us through the blood of Jesus.

Exodus 24:17 tells us that after this incident the glory of God appeared to His people. When we apply the blood of Jesus to our lives, our eyes are opened and we can see.

## Blood Covenant Today

This is exactly how the blood covenant protects us today. When the Father looks at those of us who believe in His Son, He sees the blood of Jesus over our lives. In other words, when He looks at us He sees the righteousness of Jesus! We can never be righteous—acceptable to Him—because of our own works; we are righteous only because of the blood. When God sees us—He sees the blood.

There are many powerful benefits for us due to this blood covenant. The first is protection. When we call on the name of Jesus, we are relying on the power of His blood. Thus, we can draw what I refer to as a "bloodline" that says to the enemy, "You cannot cross over this line of the blood of Jesus to attack me." This bloodline protects us from sickness and disease. The power of the blood of Jesus releases breakthrough and blessings.

Second, we are told in Leviticus 17:11 that there is life in the blood. Jesus offered up His life-giving blood for all of us. When we pray and plead the blood of Jesus, we understand that His blood is upon the doorposts of our hearts, and the spirit of death cannot defeat us. Understand that in all of these instances, the blood must still be appropriated in faith for it to become effective.

Third, the blood of Jesus gives us access to the Father. Put another way, without the shedding of blood, there is no access to the Father. Blood was required in the Old Testament so that God could dwell among His people. Today, because of our blood covenant we have through Jesus Christ, we have *immediate access* to the throne of grace.

Hebrews 10:19–20 discusses this *new and living way* to the Father that we have due to the shed blood of Christ:

> Therefore, brethren, . . . we have full freedom and confidence to enter into the [Holy of] Holies [by the power and virtue] in the blood of Jesus, by this fresh (new) and living way which He initiated and dedicated and opened for us through the separating curtain (veil of the Holy of Holies), that is, through His flesh.
>
> AMPLIFIED

Jesus was very clear about the fact that the redemption of mankind through His death on the cross was the purpose for which He came into the world. Remember, Hebrews 9:22 says that without the shedding of blood there is no remission of sins. And without the remission of sins there is no life. His purpose was also to destroy the works of the enemy—which He accomplished on the cross as well. This is the reason we can plead the blood and be protected from Satan.

Fourth is the presence of the Holy Spirit, the Comforter and Helper, who came on the Day of Pentecost, after Jesus' death, resurrection and ascension into heaven. There had to be an outpouring of the blood of Jesus before there could be an outpouring of the Holy Spirit.

Jesus desires that we share His life with Him. Thus, He instructs His followers to "drink His blood," meaning that we drink in His life and power. The blood, which we drink by faith, cleanses our sin, frees us from guilt and shame and bestows life upon us.

Peter reminds us, his readers, that we are "elect . . . unto obedience and sprinkling of the blood of Jesus Christ" (1 Peter 1:2, KJV), and that we are redeemed by the "precious blood of Christ" (verse 19).

## Moving Forward

Well, dear one, we have established every believer's connection to the covenant through the blood of Jesus. Let's continue on. You have an inheritance to claim! But first I would like to pray Hebrews 13:20–21 over your life. I believe that He will equip you with everything good:

> May the God of peace, who through the blood of the eternal covenant brought back from the dead our Lord Jesus, that great Shepherd of the sheep, equip you with everything good for doing his will, and may he work in us what is pleasing to him, through Jesus Christ, to whom be glory for ever and ever. Amen.

# — 4 —

# THE HIGHWAY OF HOLINESS

A highway shall be there, and a road, and it shall be called
the Highway of Holiness.

Isaiah 35:8, NKJV

It was time for Sunday morning worship. My normal pre-service routine involved double-checking on our worship team. I quietly pried open the door leading into the sanctuary, certain that our team was ready to begin the service. As I observed the musicians gathering at the altar, I smiled and silently prayed, *Thank You, Lord, for their faithfulness. I ask You to bless this service with Your divine presence and empower each member of the worship team to be a carrier of Your power and anointing.*

The team members were smiling and talking together animatedly as they took up their instruments and got into their places. Our worship leader checked the sound equipment.

Then with a final nod to the sound man, he turned to his keyboard in preparation for opening our corporate worship.

I returned to my office to pray with my husband, Mickey, and together we sought the Lord for His last-minute instructions. The music began. The service was beginning. The heavenlies seemed near as the air vibrated with God's glory! It was time to meet the Lord as we worshiped.

As Mickey and I entered the sanctuary and made our way down the aisle, God's presence was so strong that it swept me off my feet—literally! I found myself landing prostrate in front of the altar. I was totally captivated by the presence of the Holy Spirit; obviously He had something to reveal to me.

I was suddenly caught away in a heavenly vision and no longer aware of my natural surroundings. I still search for the adequate words to paint a picture of the majestic vision I saw.

Before my eyes, a chariot of fire swept down from the heavens. It was the most glorious sight! Flames shot out, giving the appearance of a golden glow all around the chariot as it approached. As the flames leapt out, releasing light into the atmosphere, freshly ignited flames descended from heaven to take their places, thus keeping the chariot brightly burning. Because the chariot was constantly lit with fresh fire, the brilliance never waned.

The glorious glow from the shooting flames lit a pathway, like a highway in the skies, wherever the chariot traveled. It was an eternal burning vehicle of glory.

The chariot also shone with a richness of gold that is indescribable. The depth of the golden color somehow symbolized a most profound depth of God's glory, so deep that His glory extended into eternity. Exhibiting not only the color but also the weightiness of solid gold, the chariot seemed constructed of the heaviness, the stability and the majesty of His divine glory.

The vehicle of golden fire swept through the skies as if it were circling the globe. It seemed to be searching for a landing strip. It re-circled repeatedly, finally heading toward the earth as if to land. But not landing, the fiery presence hurled itself back into the heavenlies and circled once more. Finally, the chariot of glory made a direct descent and reached the earth. I noticed that it did not actually plant firmly on the ground, but, rather, hovered a few inches above the ground. Now the chariot was directly in front of me, and I could examine its characteristics more closely.

The chariot seemed to have its own personality—that is, it appeared to be alive and active with a strong determination to move forward and accomplish its mission on the earth. Two eyes appeared on the front of the chariot, like two headlights. The eyes were focused on the ground. As I followed their gaze, I saw that the "road" beneath the hovering chariot was full of potholes and rocks. It had so many gaping gulches and deep crevices that no vehicle could travel on it. Because the road was not properly prepared for travel, the chariot seemed sad. I sensed that the chariot desired to go forth, and it grieved because there was no highway on which it could travel.

Suddenly, I knew the purpose of this vision. God was seeking a highway upon which to release His glory! I felt the compassion of the Father who desired to show His glory to His precious children, but was hindered because the pathway had not been prepared. I was overwhelmed with a sense of urgency, for I knew that He wanted to be among His people. As I continued to observe the vision, I began to cry out within myself, *Lord, how do we prepare the way? Help me to understand how to prepare You a place!*

I then saw innumerable men and women, all dressed in solid white garments, standing in rows on either side of the road. Their ranks stretched for miles. God revealed to me that these were the apostles and prophets of the Most High God. On one side of the road were the prophets, and on the opposite side were the apostles. I was amazed at the number of white-robed figures lining the road, which extended like an endless highway into mountains and plains.

A sound from the chariot caught my attention. It was the sound of a fresh burst of flames. The chariot was "firing up" to move forward. I thought to myself, *How are we going to fix this road for God's glory to travel upon it?*

Suddenly the apostles and prophets began to lie down in the road. One by one, they flung their bodies on top of the disheveled earth to fill every gulch and crevice. They did not hesitate to hurl themselves on top of sharp rocks and briars, to lay down their lives as a "highway of holiness" for the chariot of God's glory. My thoughts and emotions leaped inside me. *What bravery! What commitment! I only wish that I were that determined.*

At that moment I was overwhelmed with a sense of destiny and spiritual fortitude. I found myself involved in the sacrifice of this death-to-self experience. I quickly threw my own body down before the chariot, not caring how much pain or suffering I endured. I knew only that I wanted His glory and would gladly lay down my life for it.

Soon a level highway stretched out for the chariot to travel upon. The chariot landed on the "road" and sped forth. With a fresh thrust of fire, the chariot blazed a trail upon the new foundation of the apostles and prophets who were willing to lay down their lives for His glory.

Abruptly, I became aware of my natural surroundings; the vision was gone. Stunned by this experience, I lay unmoving on the floor, trying to gather my thoughts into some coherence. *God, does this vision mean that You are requiring more from me? How can I possibly do more? Haven't I laid down my life already for You? I feel as if I have already died a thousand times.* (Okay, I knew I was about to shift into a martyr syndrome, so I caught myself from moving into more self-pity.)

In response to my plea for understanding the vision, God spoke to me gradually, bit by bit over the next days and weeks, giving me fresh information about the blood of Jesus and its relevance for our lives. Here is a compilation of what He told me:

My desire is to move you into a greater level of My glory. The new anointing that I have for all My people will require each of them to embrace My "new thing." It is a costly anointing, and it will require a price to be paid to achieve the greater glory. The price to be paid is a commitment to give Me their very best because I have given My best—My Son!

I am going to give My children many different throne room strategies that will reveal ways to defeat their enemies and experience greater levels of My glory. They will overcome the enemy by the word of their testimony, the blood of the Lamb and not loving their own lives unto death. They will lay down their lives and be the foundation upon which I will build. I will also show My people a new structure of building, and they will have a heart to build as in the days of Nehemiah.

Because they will pay the price to change and remove themselves from an old method of building, I will release to them a new mantle of authority. This mantle will empower them with new leadership. They will become a people who embrace heaven's divine government. As they implement My government upon the earth, they will shift and align with My heavenly purposes. The new mantle will restructure their lives, their ministries, their culture, their businesses and their families. As I move My people from glory to glory, they will be changed more and more into My image.

The Lord wants us to draw closer to Him, to have fresh hunger for the revelation that will empower us to shift into His full plan for our lives. Now that we understand that we have a royal inheritance, and that we obtain it through the blood of Jesus, we next learn how to claim that inheritance. This is a walk that takes us on the highway of holiness—where we actually witness the glory of God.

I have learned that in order to achieve this, I have to remind myself continually that I am righteous and holy only because of the blood of Jesus. As I lay down my life for His glory, I can grow more and more into His image. I become, in a sense, a foundation upon which He can build.

It is a costly place of anointing, because it means we might have to change a few things about ourselves. But remember also that through the shed blood of Jesus, He offers us a new and living way. His blood releases life!

Let's review once more just how we overcome the enemy and its benefits:

> Then I heard a strong (loud) voice in heaven, saying, Now it has come—the *salvation and the power and the kingdom (the dominion, the reign)* of our God, and the *power (the sovereignty, the authority) of His Christ* (the Messiah); for the accuser of our brethren, he who keeps bringing before our God charges against them day and night, has been cast out! And they have overcome (conquered) him by means of the blood of the Lamb and by the utterance of their testimony, for they did not love and cling to life even when faced with death [holding their lives cheap till they had to die for their witnessing].
>
> Revelation 12:10–11, AMPLIFIED (emphasis added)

Our passion for the Kingdom of God and the authority to subdue the kingdoms of this world must take precedence over our personal desires.

## The Glory of the Lord

Even as I seek His glory, at the same time I do not fully understand what God's glory really represents. The word *glory* in Scripture has several different meanings. The expression of *glory* to which I refer in this book is the glory revealed when heaven touches earth, or as Bob Sorge says, "the invasion of God's reality into the human sphere" (*Glory: When Heaven Invades Earth*, Oasis House, 2002). This is when God takes His glory, which exists in heaven in divine time, pushes it through the natural atmosphere and natural time (our time on earth) and establishes the supernatural.

In other words, God takes what already exists in heaven and pushes it through the natural realm to make manifest the promise we await. I call this one of God's "suddenlies," when God releases His glory at the appointed time and "suddenly" reveals the magnificence of who He is and what He does.

A practical example is in the realm of healing. As God invades the earth with His glory, He releases what He has already written and decreed concerning healing. Then, as we mix our faith with His Word, He causes the Word to press through the natural realm to release a supernatural miracle. Hallelujah!

The Lord has already declared that all flesh shall see His glory. He is simply waiting for those who will pay the price, lay down their agendas, embrace truth and receive His glory. We discussed in the last chapter how, in Old Testament days, when blood was shed, the eyes of God's people were opened to see God's glory. Since Jesus has shed His blood—our eyes are also opened. Yes, we can witness the glory of God. We can believe that He desires to reveal it to us. The prophet Isaiah said: "The glory of the LORD will be revealed, and all mankind together will see it. For the mouth of the LORD has spoken" (Isaiah 40:5). The prophet Habakkuk said: "The earth will be filled with the knowledge of the glory of the LORD, as the waters cover the sea" (Habakkuk 2:14).

Get ready, saints! The heavens are about to invade the earth, and the whole earth will be filled with the knowledge of the glory of the Lord.

## The Kingdom Quest

Alive, active and full of power, the chariot in my vision represented God's glory being released upon the earth. Much as the written Word of God expresses "living power," so the chariot had an active part in fulfilling God's purposes on the earth.

> The chariots of God are twenty thousand, even thousands of angels: the Lord is among them, as in Sinai, in the holy place. Thou hast ascended on high, thou hast led captivity captive: thou hast received gifts for men; yea, for the rebellious also, that the LORD God might dwell among them.
>
> Psalm 68:17–18, KJV

This passage in Psalms states that when God's chariots appear, thousands of angels will come with Him. It also tells us that as He invades the earth with His glory, He leads captivity captive. In other words, at the same time God reveals His glory, thousands of angels are released to become ministering spirits to the saints upon the earth who collaborate with His plans and purposes. As a result of His glory, we are loosed from bondage, prison cell doors are opened and the oppressed are set free!

The vision of the chariot and His glory affected my life in such a dynamic way that I have been on a "Kingdom quest" ever since. I knew from the vision that I would have a part in ushering in His presence and glory in a new way; in fact, He was telling me that I would be a pioneer to help prepare the way. The process would involve a death-to-the-flesh experience. I was going to be required to press beyond my natural understanding, to renew my mind and to shift into a Kingdom mentality.

It was time to rise up to another level of spiritual maturity and authority and move past my old patterns. I know now that the highway of holiness has nothing to do with religious works, but rather with the realization that our holiness and righteousness lie solely in the finished work of Christ. Since God revealed that to me, I have been seeking the King and His Kingdom with fresh passion, more determined than ever to press into a more intimate relationship with Him.

God is not about religion; He is all about relationship. It is time for pioneering something new—a message that contains life. For me, it is a relationship with God that releases the power of the Holy Spirit, and freedom that comes only by understanding the power of the blood. Knowing I am righteous only because of the blood has freed me from a "works mentality." Keep reading—greater freedom will be yours as well.

## Wilderness Voices Preparing the Way

God is very committed to change, especially when it is we who need changing! He is invading the earth with His glory, and this invasion requires each of us to change by being prepared and matured to a new level.

But do we really desire change? As long as our lives are fine, our children are prospering, our needs are met and we are experiencing great blessing, why change? Who in his right mind wants to move away from a place of comfort and success? We may believe that we are ready to ascend to higher levels and experience the fullness of God's glory, but most of us are not fully prepared for the changes involved in getting there. It usually takes a "wilderness experience" to make us ready to change and prepare our hearts for something greater.

Two thousand years ago, heaven came to earth. Jesus left His Kingdom in heaven to be the Way. Prior to His arrival, two prophets in particular came out of the wilderness to prepare for His coming glory. Isaiah addressed this through his prophetic message, and then John the Baptist picked up where Isaiah left off. The prophets passed the baton in the spiritual race toward God's fullness; yet most of the people who heard the Good News were too bound in religious tradition to receive it and were, therefore, unprepared for change.

Let's read the truths that Isaiah declared and compare them with the words of John the Baptist:

> A voice of one calling: "In the desert prepare the way for the LORD; make straight in the wilderness a highway for our God. Every valley shall be raised up, every mountain and hill made low; the rough ground shall become level, the rugged places a plain. And the glory of the LORD will be revealed, and all mankind together will see it. For the mouth of the LORD has spoken."
>
> Isaiah 40:3–5

> In those days John the Baptist came, preaching in the Desert of Judea and saying, "Repent, for the kingdom of heaven is near." This is he who was spoken of through the prophet Isaiah: "A voice of one calling in the desert, 'Prepare the way for the Lord, make straight paths for him.'"
>
> Matthew 3:1–3

Both prophets were ministering words that indicated change. Both were crying out from wilderness places. And both declared that a way needed to be prepared for God's glory. Notice that Isaiah specifically mentions making a "highway for our God."

We can learn a great deal about preparing the way for God's glory by studying these two Scripture passages:

1. God first builds a highway in our hearts.
2. He then fills in the valleys of our hearts.
3. He examines our hearts and tears down every high place—every area in which our hearts do not put Him first.
4. He makes every crooked path straight.
5. He causes every rough place to be made smooth.
6. Then we lay down our lives for Him, for we must decrease so that He might increase.

Our mandate in this season is to receive the clarion call to be those who prepare the way! Let's pick up the baton, receiving the prophetic challenge to be among those who are not only prepared themselves, but also preparing a way for others to receive God's glory.

Just as these prophets faced opposition, we also will be persecuted. They confronted a religious structure, a belief system and man's tradition. They preached boldly a "straight path" message, which involved traveling a highway of holiness. Theirs were voices that the Lord used to prepare the way for a greater dimension of His glory on the earth.

Will you also be a voice?

## Straight Paths and Smooth Edges

*Strong's* lexicon tells us that the Hebrew word for *make straight* in the previous Isaiah passage means "to be straight, right, upright, pleasing, good." Another passage, Proverbs

3:5–6, tells us that it is God Himself who straightens out our paths as we trust in Him: "Trust in the LORD with all your heart and lean not on your own understanding; in all your ways acknowledge him, and he will make your paths straight." When we trust Him totally and embrace His direction for our lives—and that means leaving the past behind and following Him—He is committed to "straightening" us out.

When God says that every mountain will be brought low, He is referring to every high thing in our lives that He has set His face against, such as pride, competition, self-promotion, our own will, our private agendas, our personal ambitions and so on. In other words, He is committed to bringing these things down.

Making the rough places smooth refers to our "rough edges." Do you have any of these? My goodness, I do! Most of us are keen at noticing the rough edges of others, but it is time to examine our own rough places. When things "get rough," then we can really tell if we have any "rough edges." Tough times expose tough hearts.

God desires to fill in every valley. Each low place in our hearts will be filled to overflowing by His love and His Spirit. Every deep crevice of pain, shameful memories and devastation will be full of His glory as He heals us from the past. Every deep canyon in our lives will become a positive confession of "I can do all things through Christ who strengthens me!" And "What the enemy has meant for harm, God has turned around for my good!"

Is there any area in your heart that has become hardened toward the plans of God? Do you feel you have stepped out in faith only to fail? Take courage! His highway of holiness is a highway of restoration. God has been preparing us for the fullness of His glory. As we receive, we in turn prepare others. If you are ready to shift out of an old place of despair, then allow Him to prepare you for the new place that He has provided for you.

## Satan Twists the Straight Paths

Let me add a warning here: The enemy desires to twist every step we take. Satan wants to hinder us from receiving the free flow of God's Spirit and glory. He blinds our eyes so we are unable to see the truth, and plugs up our ears so we cannot hear it.

He also persecutes the saints with religious opposition and false accusations. A "religious spirit" attempts to hinder the glorious release of signs, wonders and miracles. This spirit twists the truth concerning present-day revelation and the different ministries of the Holy Spirit. The religious spirit causes many of God's people to cling to old doctrine, remain in religious comfort zones and reject all present truth concerning God's divine movement upon the earth.

Never let yourself be deceived by a religious spirit, but rather be determined to be open-minded to the revelation of truth. We cannot assume that we know everything about God or even how He desires to move. He is doing a "new thing." (For more information on the religious spirit, see my book *Destiny Thieves: Defeat Seducing Spirits and Achieve Your Purpose in God*, Chosen Books, 2007.)

God is requiring each of us to rise to a higher level. Many spiritual pioneers are actively pursuing God's presence and glory. They are not allowing the religious spirit to trap them. Tossing tradition to the side, they are moving beyond man's mind-sets while seeking the fullness of His Spirit.

Will you join them? Will you become one of God's soldiers who will lay down personal ambition, the fear of failure and the fear of being different? Will you step into the unknown?

## Celebrate the Changes

God has been reordering and restructuring my life for as long as I can remember. And yet, all along He has remained faithful to lead me on paths that release increase and enlargement.

I have learned to celebrate the changes God has required of me. At times, even though I know better, I still fight hard to hold on to what is traditional and comfortable. But He is faithful to confront me with a new way—a living way—and His truth concerning my future. Each change has been coupled with greater dependence on His Holy Spirit, and I grow stronger with each transition. I love what Dr. Wanda Turner says in her book *Celebrate Change* (Treasure House, 2001): "Mountains pack their bags when they see me coming!"

As an added blessing, the Father has remained committed to conforming me into the image of His Son. After all, is that not what this life is all about—being changed into His image, making a difference and experiencing Him? As we move forward, we are walking in our destinies and possessing our promises—and we are learning about those very things. But our fulfillment is achieved only if we are on the correct highway—the "high way," the higher highway that leads to a greater level of His glory.

This involves doing business His way, holding church services His way and seeking Him His way. It is time to rid ourselves of religious tradition and legalism. God is true to His plan, and He does have a way in which He demands things be done. Those of us who attempt to do Kingdom business the same as usual soon will discover that God has decided to get a new partner. He refuses to act without man, but He works alongside man only as long as He chooses in order to bring about His divine plan.

Let me invite you to make a decision to change and to walk this highway with me. Yes, there will be seasons when we advance into unknown territory. As God rids us of legalism and strict adherence to the Law of the Old Testament, trying to make things right in our own strength, we will gain greater understanding of His grace. And, even though we are required to lay down our lives for Him, He repays the sacrifice with expansion and enlargement. He will visit and commune with us while guiding us into truth. Hallelujah!

Look further at the way Isaiah describes this highway that the Lord has prepared:

> The wilderness and the solitary place shall be glad for them; and the desert shall rejoice, and blossom as the rose. It shall blossom abundantly, and rejoice even with joy and singing: the glory of Lebanon shall be given unto it, the excellency of Carmel and Sharon, they shall see the glory of the Lord, and the excellency of our God.
>
> Strengthen ye the weak hands, and confirm the feeble knees. Say to them that are of a fearful heart, Be strong, fear not: behold, your God will come with vengeance, even God with a recompense; he will come and save you.
>
> Then the eyes of the blind shall be opened, and the ears of the deaf shall be unstopped. Then shall the lame man leap as an hart, and the tongue of the dumb sing: for in the wilderness shall waters break out, and streams in the desert. And the parched ground shall become a pool, and the thirsty land springs of water: in the habitation of dragons, where each lay, shall be grass with reeds and rushes.
>
> And an highway shall be there, and a way, and it shall be called The way of holiness; the unclean shall not pass over it; but it shall be for those: the wayfaring men, though fools, shall not err therein.
>
> No lion shall be there, nor any ravenous beast shall go up thereon, it shall not be found there; but the redeemed shall walk there: And the ransomed of the Lord shall return, and come to Zion with songs and everlasting joy upon their heads:

they shall obtain joy and gladness, and sorrow and sighing shall flee away.

Isaiah 35, KJV

Even when the road that God has us travel is difficult, look at the outcome for those who keep moving forward: The highway of holiness is a road of abundance, excellence and healing. We need not be fearful-hearted (the opposite of brave-hearted). We can be strong and courageous because God will protect us with a vengeance. As we travel on God's highway, we will have open eyes and ears to see and hear Him by the Spirit, and we will go forth with joy and singing.

Read Isaiah 35 again and envision yourself traveling God's highway with a brave heart. Take some time to meditate on all the positives along the highway of holiness. Then read it again and boldly declare all that God has prepared for you as you travel His highway.

### Positive Confession for the Future

At this point, we need to take some time to stop and pray. It is very important to make positive confessions concerning claiming your inheritance. As you pray this prayer, which is based on Isaiah 35, you will override any negative words spoken about your future—by you or anyone else. We will plead the blood of Jesus and draw a bloodline so that the enemy cannot steal your blessings. This prayer will drive out fear and empower you with courage and bravery to face your future and receive God's abundant blessings:

*Lord, as I travel Your highway of holiness, I am confident that You have prepared a highway of life. Although at times I may feel lonely and weak, You have promised to strengthen my feeble knees. If I am fearful, then You encourage me by stating that I need not fear. I am empowered to become strong because You will come with a mighty vengeance and save me from my enemies.*

*Even when I know I am experiencing a wilderness season, the roses will continue to bloom, and You will place joy in my heart because You love me with everlasting love. I am confident that this way of holiness will become lasting springs of water as You purify my thoughts, deeds and actions.*

*I am thankful for the blood of Jesus that cleanses me. I plead the blood of Jesus over my life and my body. I draw a bloodline that will completely halt the enemy. I am confident that when Jesus shed His precious blood at the cross, it gave me access to the throne room. I can cast all my cares on You, Lord.*

*As You continue to sanctify my motives and circumcise my heart anew, I know that You will provide pools of refreshing and draw me ever closer to Yourself. You have promised to protect me from the lion that seeks to destroy me and fools who attempt to deceive me as I travel this pathway of holiness. I will come to Zion, the City of God, with songs of joy and gladness, and all sorrow and sighing will flee away. I pray this prayer in Jesus' name, Amen.*

Let's travel His higher way, the highway of holiness. It is holiness that comes from being One with Christ—not holiness based on anything that you and I can accomplish. Though the pathways might require time spent before His throne in prayer and supplication, I can promise that you will be amazed by the life-giving and freeing power of the blood of Jesus.

# — 5 —

# WE NEED TO SEE!

The Spirit of the Sovereign LORD is on me, because the LORD
has anointed me to preach good news to the poor. . . . They
will be called oaks of righteousness, a planting of the LORD
for the display of his splendor.

Isaiah 61:1, 3

Have you ever told God that you need to see where you
are going? Leaving the past behind means entering into
unknown territory, and walking into unknown territory is
difficult. But leaving familiar surroundings and comfort zones
is necessary when God requires we embrace a new thing or
a fresh direction.

I am a person of certainty. I thrive on being sure, steadfast and steady. I also have a need to know. In other words,
when I am sure and I know the details concerning a task or
project, I am empowered to move forward. When I do not

know in advance what is expected of me, however, I fret and worry unnecessarily. I become stuck, and, therefore, unfruitful, whenever I am unsure of the situation.

When we step onto the highway of holiness—walking in faith and trusting Him in all situations—most of the time we are unsure because we do not know the outcome or full direction of His plan. The faith walk is the process of traveling on an unknown and challenging road. That is why it is a walk of faith! Although it can be a difficult road to travel, it is a necessary way that builds godly character and greater faith. Walking into unknown territory is part of the process of developing our faith as well as experiencing supernatural breakthroughs.

## Abraham: The One Who Crossed Over

Abraham understood what it means to walk into unknown territory. He left his birthplace to heed God's call to enter into a Promised Land. How did Abraham, who did not have a clue where he was headed, remain steadfast?

Abraham crossed over. He had to "come over" in order to "overcome" any possible fears or doubts he had concerning his future. Abraham was human, and I am sure that it was difficult for him emotionally as well as physically to leave behind all that was familiar and walk out his destiny. Getting to the other side of emotions can be so challenging that we often choose not to let go of the past. Pressing beyond our emotions is a "crossover" point for all of us during our faith walk.

Abraham was a man of faith because of his ability not to focus on the challenges he saw before him in the natural, but rather to keep his eyes on what he knew God had told him in the supernatural. He developed the ability to see beyond what he was experiencing. This is an attribute we all need in order to follow the Lord into the unknown. Like Abraham, we must trust that God is leading in the realm of the supernatural and not be motivated by what we feel or see in the natural.

On top of the challenge of leaving the old life behind in order to enter into his destiny, Abraham had a second area to work through: family issues with his nephew Lot.

You may be familiar with the biblical account of Lot and how he chose to live in Sodom, one of the "twin cities of sin." Emotions wreak havoc when a family member chooses to live in sin; and yet Abraham knew that he had to keep moving forward in order to fulfill his divine destiny. When Lot's household was captured by four neighboring kings, Abraham came to the rescue to deliver Lot's family from slavery. It was at this time in Abraham's life that he was referred to as the "Hebrew" (Genesis 14:13) or "one who crosses over."

It is important to understand the connection between Abraham's "crossing over" and his putting on a warfare mantle for his family. It is tied directly to the significance of covenant relationship. Members of natural, blood-related families, as well as the family of God, are covenant-related. Abraham understood the significance of covenant and, therefore, went to war on his nephew's behalf.

It is the same with the Church. We in the Body of Christ are blood-related because of the blood of Jesus. We are, therefore, in covenant with the Lord and with each other. We must understand how important our covenant relationship is with the Lord and never treat it lightly. For His part, the Lord will war on our behalf. He has promised to go to battle for us, going ahead of us to defeat our enemies. Our part in keeping covenant with God is to continue to "cross over" into every new place where the Lord instructs us to go. This is how we move forward from glory to glory. We will never stop crossing over; it is a progression of breakthroughs as we step up one level, or revelation at a time, and move on to the next.

Because Abraham was the father of many nations and our spiritual father, I believe that what he possessed and experienced during his walk of faith and obedience affects our inheritance and destiny today. Spiritually we are Abraham's family (he is the father of our faith), and when he went to battle for the destiny of Lot, he also warred over our destiny. In other words, when he warred against the four kings, he battled for his natural seed as well as his future spiritual seed—us!

## Four "Kings" That Steal Our Inheritance

As we follow the steps Abraham took to possess his inheritance, we gain fresh strategies for possessing our own inheritance. By studying the names of the four kings that Abraham battled in order to save Lot and his family, and by examining the names of each king's dominion (all documented in Genesis 14:9), we gain important insight into the strategy of the enemy, as well as the strategies we can use to battle for our own inheritance and walk forward in faith. (I am indebted to Cornwall and Smith's *Exhaustive Dictionary*, *Enhanced Strong's Lexicon* and *Strong's Concordance* for many of the following definitions.)

### The King of Elam: Kedorlaomer

- *His name:* The name *Kedorlaomer* means "to bind sheaves." This implies "binding up."
- *His dominion:* Kedorlaomer ruled in Elam, which means "eternity."
- *The strategy of the spirit associated with the king:* The spirit of Elam desires to imprison by binding up

with cords, or to bind so that one is unable to move forward. This strategy implies that we can be bound to our past, meaning that the enemy uses emotions, fear, sickness and other strongholds to keep us from moving forward. The word *bind* also implies a "bent mind." Some of us are bent in the wrong direction in our thinking concerning God's delivering power and His ability to heal and restore. The enemy hopes to keep us bound up eternally.

- *Our strategy:* If we rely on our natural senses and natural understanding, then we will remain bound. It is time to shift into the supernatural. As we plead the blood of Jesus, we are being loosed from the clutches of the enemy. Oh, thank the Lord for the power of His blood!

### The King of Nations (Goiim): Tidal

- *His name:* The name *Tidal* means "terrible, great fear, to make afraid" and to cause to "shrink back and crawl away." The name *Tidal* is associated with the word *serpent*, which is another word for divination and witchcraft.

- *His dominion:* He was the king of nations. This implies that this spirit today is a territorial stronghold; it wields demonic influence over large amounts of territory. The word *nations* in this passage not only refers to people, but also is used figuratively as a "swarm of locusts."

- *The strategy of the spirit associated with the king:* Tidal attempts to make us so fearful that we shrink back from the warfare needed to win the victory. This occult spirit also hides the truth from us so that when we are longing to see and receive revelation, it is hidden. This stronghold attempts to exalt itself in our eyes. Like a swarm of locusts, it will devour our future if we believe the lies of our enemy.

• *Our strategy:* As we press into the supernatural, we must take care not to shrink back in fear. The serpent spirit speaks lies; we must not believe them. We must learn to use supernatural vision and depend wholeheartedly upon the Spirit of God and what He says about our future. As we draw a bloodline by the Spirit, the enemy will not be able to terrorize us and cause us to shrink back from our destiny. Let's lay hold of the promises right now—we can have them because of the shed blood of Jesus.

### The King of Shinar: Amraphel

• *His name:* The name *Amraphel* means "sayer of darkness."
• *His dominion:* Shinar was the ancient name for the territory known as Babylon. The city of Babylon stood on the Euphrates River, and it is believed to be where the Tower of Babel stood. Like the language of Babel, the name *Babylon* means "mixed and confused." Today Babylon is symbolic of the world system. This spirit encompasses all that is evil upon the earth, especially when referring to the economic system. The love of money and its evil influence are connected to the spirit of Babylon.
• *The strategy of the spirit associated with the king:* Amraphel, king of Shinar, speaks darkness into every structure of influence. There will never be hope in his words. Most of us are at war against the evil effects of the Babylon spirit. The stronghold is like an octopus, wrapping its demonic tentacles around businesses, corporations, governments, school systems, churches and families. This spirit, for instance, has robbed educational structures by infiltrating them with ungodly perspectives, and it

has decimated the family structure by the "convenience" of abortion.

- *Our strategy:* Like Abraham, we must cross over into warfare against this demonic, destructive spirit. Overthrowing its influence will require words of faith and declaring God's life over the death structures it has influenced. Once again, it may appear as if we are losing the battle, but with supernatural vision, we will see the victory. We must protect ourselves by listening only to what God says concerning our future. Remember, we are partakers of the Abrahamic covenant. We have the same inheritance as he had.

### The King of Ellasar: Arioch

- *His name:* The name *Arioch* means "lion-like."
- *His dominion:* Ellasar was a town in Babylon; once again, it represents the principalities of Babylon. I find it interesting that the name *Ellasar* actually translates as "God is the chastener."
- *The strategy of the spirit associated with the king:* The strategy of Ellasar is to raise its head as a roaring lion that attempts to steal, kill and destroy.
- *Our strategy:* This enemy will attempt to sound like the roar of the Lion of Judah. As we cross over into our inheritance, we must not listen to him, for his is a false sound. Although the devil will roar over our circumstances to make us fear and back off from our crossover point, we must continue forward, knowing that the Lord has gone before us and has already defeated our enemies. Ultimately, as we cross over into our destinies using our supernatural eyesight, God will chasten our enemies. Do not follow the words you hear in the natural realm. Trust in the Spirit of the Lord.

Jesus is a Lion and also a Lamb. He is the Lamb that was slain so that we could claim our destinies. Thank the Lord once more for His blood that empowers you to claim your inheritance and your future.

Do you see how examining the names of these four kings gives us insight into our enemy's strategies? And do you see that we can glean strategies from that insight for fighting our battles more effectively so that our highway is made less rough? Yes, it is a difficult road to travel, and, yes, it is a road leading often into the unknown, but our God gives us the tools necessary to build our character and faith and enable us to walk on it in victory. We can rejoice in the knowledge that the blood of Jesus opens our eyes to His truths—and gives us complete victory as we heed His Word.

Now, are you ready to possess some ground in the Spirit? I know you are because you are destined to possess your promises! Let's continue on.

## We Need His Sevenfold Spirit

In order to pursue the inheritance God has for each of us, we need to see the fullness of God's Spirit operating in our lives. The book of Isaiah reveals the sevenfold Spirit of God. Let's examine this passage as a foundation for further understanding the seven attributes of His Spirit:

A shoot will come up from the stump of Jesse; from his roots a Branch will bear fruit. The Spirit of the LORD will rest on him—the Spirit of wisdom and of understanding, the Spirit of counsel and of power, the Spirit of knowledge and of the fear of the LORD—and he will delight in the fear of the LORD.

He will not judge by what he sees with his eyes, or decide by what he hears with his ears; but with righteousness he will judge the needy, with justice he will give decisions for the poor of the earth. He will strike the earth with the rod of his mouth; with the breath of his lips he will slay the wicked.

Isaiah 11:1–4

This passage is a prophetic word about the coming of Jesus and His divine attributes. These attributes, outlined in the Isaiah passage, are that the Spirit of the Lord would rest on Him, and that He would have wisdom, understanding, counsel, might, knowledge and the fear of the Lord. By His blood, we are one with Christ; therefore, the attributes of the sevenfold Spirit of God are ours, bestowed like a mantle of divine authority upon every believer.

### The First Attribute: The Spirit of the Lord Himself

Let's start with the first attribute of God, which is available to every believer. It is the Spirit of the Lord Himself. It may sound a bit confusing that one of the attributes of the sevenfold Spirit of God is the Spirit of the Lord. That sounds redundant. But Scripture is clear that the "Spirit of the Lord" coming down to rest upon a person is an actual gift that God imparts to His chosen ones.

Isaiah 11:1 says that Jesus, the Branch, grew from the root of Jesse, meaning that He was a descendant of Jesse (Jesse was King David's father). The name *Jesse* is translated as "I possess." The spiritual DNA of Christ involved possessing a promise. It is the very same DNA that each of us inherits—a determination and divine grace to possess all that the Father has for us.

Verse 2 states that the Spirit of the Lord rested upon Christ. The word *Lord* is from the name *Jehovah*, which, as we discussed earlier, means "God Almighty" or "the all-existing

One." The name in its fullness also means "to come to pass, to cause to bring about and to happen."

This tells us that Jehovah is the God of our future. He is not only all-existing, but He also causes our words of promise to manifest. And along with that is the power to become. Wow! This means that we have been given the power to become the sons and daughters of God and, therefore, to take our rightful places and receive our full inheritance.

When the Spirit of the Lord (Jehovah) came upon Jesus, supernatural empowerment rested upon Him to fulfill His destiny. It is the very same with each of us. Because we have received Him, He has given us the "power to become the sons of God" and fulfill our destinies:

> He came unto his own, and his own received him not. But as many as received him, to them gave he power to become the sons of God, even to them that believe on his name: which were born, not of blood, nor of the will of the flesh, nor of the will of man, but of God.
>
> John 1:11–13, KJV

Along with that "power to become" is a bestowment of the fullness of God to accomplish whatever is needed for any given situation.

When the Spirit of the Lord comes upon us, we are empowered to do great exploits. His Spirit rests upon us like a mantle of authority and power. The word *upon* actually means that something comes "on" us to take us "up." In other words, this part of His character empowers us to come up to another level. Just as heaven comes to earth when we pray, so we rise up to meet heaven and come into agreement with His will and Word.

When the fullness of the Spirit of the Lord falls upon us, we can exhibit the various attributes of His sevenfold Spirit, such as prophecy (revelation), wisdom and might. Scripture gives us vivid examples of the sevenfold attributes of God's Spirit empowering the saints.

When the Spirit of the Lord fell upon King Saul, for example, he prophesied. This happened to Saul twice as he came into the company of prophets. He gained a supernatural ability to receive revelation, to see into the Spirit and to move in a gift of prophecy. (See 1 Samuel 10:11; 19:23.)

Gideon also was empowered by the Spirit of the Lord. When neighboring enemies of the Israelites began to join forces and camped in a nearby valley, the Spirit of the Lord guided Gideon to blow his trumpet. The supernatural sound summoned an army that defeated their longtime enemies. (See Judges 6:34.)

The Spirit of the Lord came upon David when Samuel anointed him as the next king: "So Samuel took the horn of oil and anointed him in the presence of his brothers, and from that day on the Spirit of the LORD came upon David in power" (1 Samuel 16:13). At that point, David was established as the next king of Israel. Every challenge he faced thereafter prepared him to rule and reign. David was able to defeat Goliath and lead armies into battle all because he was under the Spirit of might (one of God's sevenfold attributes). Later, other attributes of God's sevenfold Spirit manifested to empower David, such as the Spirit of counsel and the Spirit of wisdom.

Judges 13:25 describes how the Spirit of the Lord also was upon Samson. He had supernatural strength under the mantle of the Lord's Spirit and His might.

The Word says that we can have the very same Spirit of the Lord upon us as we are transformed into His image and move from glory to glory: "But we all, with open face beholding as in a glass the glory of the Lord, are changed into the same image from glory to glory, even as by the Spirit of the Lord" (2 Corinthians 3:18, KJV). In fact, in order to move from one level of glory to the next level, we need the fullness of the Spirit of the Lord operating in our lives.

### The Second Attribute: The Spirit of Wisdom

The second attribute of the sevenfold Spirit of God is God's wisdom. Praying for knowledge of God's perfect will is important, but we also need wisdom—divine insight and proper spiritual judgment—in order to implement it.

The word *wisdom* is a Hebrew word that means not only having wisdom, but also being wise and skillful in warfare, administration and religious affairs. This is exciting because it means we can depend upon God's Spirit of wisdom to teach us the skills we need for spiritual warfare.

Because God's wisdom is different from natural wisdom, we must touch heaven to receive His divine wisdom for our spiritual battles. Otherwise, we are simply "beating the air" with no direction or strategy, about which the apostle Paul speaks (see 1 Corinthians 9:26). Fighting a war with no divine strategy or direction is similar to a boxer beating the air and never striking the opponent. Can you imagine going into warfare and simply waving our arms in the air? How effective would that be? The enemy most likely would wonder if we were ever going to throw a solid punch! Precious saint, it is time to touch heaven so we can become effective warriors.

King Solomon is perhaps the best example in the Bible of a man being empowered by God's wisdom and knowledge. Rather than asking God for riches, wealth and honor, Solomon asked for wisdom and knowledge so that he could properly judge the people. This pleased the Lord, so He bestowed upon Solomon great wisdom (see 2 Chronicles

1:10–12). God's wisdom instructed Solomon as he built the Lord's Temple and later guided the worship.

As we approach the end times, we must receive a greater measure of God's wisdom so that we build our "temples"—our earthly bodies—to house His glory and so that our worship is led by His Spirit.

The Lord also desires to equip us with His divine administrative skills, which empower our businesses, churches and ministries. Because He is bound to His covenant promises, His heart's desire is to give us everything needed to ensure our success.

As we venture into unknown territory, we cannot depend upon wisdom that was learned during a past season or else we will be using antiquated weapons. Crossing over into our land of promise requires freshly sharpened weapons. Sharpened spiritual discernment, wisdom and understanding the mechanics of spiritual warfare are needed in this season. Depending upon God's Spirit of wisdom ensures our victory in our new places of authority.

### The Third Attribute: The Spirit of Understanding

Wisdom is closely connected to the next attribute of God's Spirit: understanding. In fact, we cannot have understanding if we do not first have a measure of wisdom and operate with spiritual discernment. Otherwise, our understanding is based upon the intellect rather than the Spirit of God.

This means allowing the Holy Spirit to teach us—even if His leading appears to be the opposite of what we already believe! Yes, doctrines of man will hinder the knowledge and understanding God desires to give us. Jesus referred to the Pharisees as blind. This is because they held tightly to their legalistic, manmade ideas and doctrines. God desires to reveal mysteries to us, but we cannot understand them unless we are willing to let go of what we think we already know. When God releases divine revelation He shows us what has been hidden—or not understood. Revelation will come whenever we choose to allow our doctrines to be proven wrong.

It is all right to back up for a minute and re-read what I just wrote. I had to chew on it for a while when the Lord spoke it to me. Are we truly willing to admit we might be wrong? Only then can we embrace the Spirit of wisdom and understanding. Divine revelation brings with it the anointing for us to receive its truth. We can therefore "know" and "understand," for eyes that were once blind are opened to see Him as He is.

Think, for example, of the reaction of the people around Jesus when He said that they must "drink" His blood. The New Testament describes how the people were offended at this saying. The Church did not comprehend this until the Holy Spirit came to earth and released the revelation concerning the importance of Jesus' blood.

Trying to understand what God is doing without His attribute of understanding causes us to reason solely with our minds, our intellects. If we form opinions based on our intellect alone, we will not grasp the spiritual dynamics of all that God is saying and doing. We cannot judge properly with the natural eye because God moves by our faith. Plus, He is doing things behind the scenes that we are unable to see at the time.

God has promised to give us acute spiritual discernment—the same that Christ had. Jesus knew when the Pharisees had ulterior motives, and He was empowered to judge properly the motives of others' hearts. He also had the ability to discern the demonic spirits that were oppressing the people around Him. His disciples operated in that same power.

We need this empowerment, as well, and God has promised to equip us with this attribute of His Spirit. As we pray for heaven to come to earth, aligning ourselves with God's perfect will, we need greater measures of spiritual discernment in order to provide us with greater understanding.

### The Fourth Attribute: The Spirit of Counsel

The Spirit of counsel is the attribute of God that involves His godly direction and instruction. As you know, there is counsel from man and then there is divine counsel, which comes only from the Father. We need both, but Proverbs 19:21 states that although many plans are in a man's heart, only God's counsel will ultimately stand.

Approaching God in intimate relationship positions us properly to receive His divine direction, correction and instruction. It is in this intimate place that He reveals the purpose for His plans. This is where our "whys" get answered.

His counsel is similar to a blood transfusion. He not only loves us, but provides us with a life-giving flow that sets us back on track with our destiny. No longer are we striving to please man. Rather, we rest in His divine direction for our lives. As He counsels us, we gain renewed purpose and vision, which propel us to achieve our destiny.

When faced with the destruction caused by the Amalekites, King David sought God's divine counsel for his warfare strategy. David asked the Lord for guidance, and God's answer was "Pursue: for thou shalt surely overtake them, and without fail and recover all" (1 Samuel 30:8, KJV).

In the natural scheme of things, David might not have been so bold to step out on God's leading. All the women and children, including those in his entire household, had been taken captive by the Amalekites. The men in his army were ready to stone him. But with the Spirit of God upon him, David followed the Lord's instructions, plundered the enemy's camp and recovered all that was stolen. God's Spirit gave him wise counsel.

As we move forward in this troubled world, we have to trust in His ability to lead. Places where we have not ventured to carry the Gospel have opened, and we have new spiritual trails to follow. We are being commanded to think outside our religious "boxes" so that we can move by God's Spirit. If we have ever needed His counsel, dear one, it is now!

### The Fifth Attribute: The Spirit of Might

The word *might* is a Hebrew word that means "strength, valor and bravery." It is further explained as "mighty deeds." How can we possibly do the mighty deeds, or greater things, as Jesus instructed, unless we have the Spirit of might operating in and through us?

The more we pray for heaven to touch the earth, the more we will be challenged with opposition from religious spirits. Religious spirits hindered even the work of Jesus when He was in Nazareth:

> And they took offense at him. Jesus said to them, "Only in his hometown, among his relatives and in his own house is a prophet without honor." He could not do any miracles there, except lay his hands on a few sick people and heal them. And he was amazed at their lack of faith.
>
> Mark 6:3–6

If a religious structure could prevent moves of the miraculous through Christ, just imagine how much these hindering spirits adversely affect our faith today. Pressing past all the religious spirits that come against us requires tremendous courage. As we receive His mantle of might and power—which we can receive only by faith—the Lord promises to release His grace.

### The Sixth Attribute: The Spirit of Knowledge

As I began to search for the full interpretation of the word *knowledge* as one of the sevenfold attributes of God, I was amazed at how often the word *know* appears in Scripture. The Lord wants us to know many things—particularly to know how, when and where to acquire knowledge.

Knowledge is key for us humans so that we can make proper decisions. If we want to avoid failure, we seek to know how to do something well. If we want to walk securely into the future, we seek prophetic insight to gain hope and courage to fulfill our destiny. If we are facing death, we search the Word of God and quote Scriptures concerning healing and life. We gain knowledge so that we *know*.

Too often we take the wrong road in the "knowing" process by always needing to know the answers. This can easily lead us to want to control the future. How are we seduced by this evil? By seeking answers from ungodly sources or seeking counselors who will give us the answers we desire to hear. I have witnessed many saints who received godly counsel and godly direction, but it was not the "word" they desired to hear. So, in an attempt to control, they sought counsel that would agree with their decisions and behavior patterns. (We discuss dangers of "the need to know" more in a moment.)

We might not always be given insight. If God is not enlightening us concerning a certain situation, He is most likely leading us to trust Him in that new season. In that case, we will not "know," but we are still required to trust and follow. Once again, needing always to know will open doors to the voice of the enemy and the occult. Be careful not to fall into this snare of the enemy.

God has promised to place upon us the mantle of His Spirit of knowledge. In fact, as He makes Himself known to us, He is empowering us with knowledge. As we align ourselves properly with His will and pray that His will be done on earth as it is in heaven, we will begin to know Him at a deeper level. As a result, more of His knowledge will be imparted to us.

As the glory of God is released, we receive knowledge about it; that is the reason for this season in which heaven is invading earth: "For the earth will be filled with the knowledge of the glory of the LORD, as the waters cover the sea" (Habakkuk 2:14).

The tribe of Issachar was gifted with understanding and with knowledge of the times and seasons of the Lord. This is an attribute that each of us can have today. Understanding that we live in the end times and knowing our place on the wall—our battle station—will empower us to become effective warriors.

God opens doors of opportunity during certain time frames, and these opportunities come and go quickly. The Lord desires to give us what we need to shift into fruitfulness and fulfillment. As heaven touches earth, expect to become more empowered with His divine knowledge about all that concerns you.

### *The Seventh Attribute: The Fear of the Lord*

We have studied six of the seven attributes of God: the Spirit of God Himself as He comes upon a person to empower him or her, wisdom, understanding, counsel, might and knowledge. The last attribute concerning the sevenfold Spirit of God is the fear of the Lord. The Word states that God did not give us a spirit of fear. Rather, He has given us a spirit of power, love and a sound mind (see 2 Timothy

1:7). The fear of the Lord, therefore, is not the same as a spirit of fear.

There is fear that torments, and that fear is from Satan. If you suffer anguish, terror and torment, then there is a demonic assignment against you. Conversely, there is fear that is healthy, reverent awe of God. The Lord will not torment us with fear. The fear of the Lord is being conscious of sin. It is the understanding and awareness of His desire for holiness and righteousness, and it always includes a deep desire to repent.

All too often, we take the Lord for granted. During church services, many have abandoned holy reverence of the Lord's presence. Although we are not to become "spooky spiritual," there is a degree of respect and admiration that should be voluntary when we witness the Lord's anointing and presence.

I wonder how often we grieve the Holy Spirit, who wants to commune with us. We are His Bride, and He requires intimacy, yet we are too preoccupied with how long the service is, what we were doing the day before and what we will be doing later in the day. We are caught up with the cares of life and forget that He is waiting to speak to us. Giving someone time says to that person that he or she is valued. How much do we honestly value the Lord?

If I go for long periods without studying the Word, I become fearful. I am not afraid that I will be punished (that is an unhealthy and unjustified fear), but I am concerned that I will miss out on what He desires to speak. I need my daily manna, a fresh word from Him, so that I am empowered to fulfill His will for my life. If I am not seeking Him daily, then I am taking Him for granted. I need to be in awe of Him.

We also need to be mindful that we are to stand in awe of His marvelous works. Nehemiah speaks of the terribleness of God: "I beseech thee, O LORD God of heaven, the great and terrible God, that keepeth covenant and mercy for them that love him and observe his commandments" (Nehemiah 1:5, KJV). The passage is speaking of this "terrible" attribute in the sense of our having awe and reverence before Him because of the power and might of His character.

It is spiritually healthy to fear the Lord because of His greatness. Are you glad that He keeps His covenant with you and promises to show forth His love and mercy? He promises to do this if we are faithful to fulfill our part, which is to love Him and observe His commandments.

If we do not possess a reverential fear of the Lord, we will become easy prey for the enemy. God promises that He will manifest Himself in a greater way, exposing all lack of reverence and respect for His Word and His presence. He promises to keep us on the right road, following the right Spirit—His Holy Spirit—by turning up the fire that keeps us all in line. He loves us that much.

## The Dangers of Wanting to Know

Most of us have failed in our efforts to be led by the sevenfold Spirit of God. I want to look a little more closely at the attribute of knowledge, because this is where so many people go astray. At times I have gotten in such a spiritual tizzy about the unknown that I have opened the door to a demonic attack. Were you aware that always having to know who, what, where, when, why and how because you mistrust God and His Word releases a witchcraft assignment against us?

You may recall that the root of the word *serpent* is linked to the words for "divination" and "the need to know." Divination involves any attempt to know the future through occult measures. These include horoscopes, crystal balls, Ouija boards, tarot cards, fortune-tellers and psychics—even when used as "parlor games."

There is nothing innocent or safe about the occult. Scripture prohibits any form of divination; we must study the Word of the Lord when we desire to know His plans for our lives. Many people, however—and this includes believers—seek out spirits of divination through these demonic means. If we become impatient with God's timing and look for answers to His mysteries apart from Him, then we are releasing the assignment of witchcraft against us.

Witchcraft and divination are connected with the occult. Remember, the word *occult* means "hidden." The purpose of occult spirits is to keep the truth hidden from us. The Lord may deliberately choose not to reveal things to us so that our faith is developed. If we resist Him and have such a need to know that we pursue occult means to satisfy our murmuring and complaining, then the enemy seduces us by pretending to reveal truth but actually deceives us and leads us into darkness. This ungodly seeking and the resultant deception could become a never-ending cycle if we resist God and embrace demonic strategies.

In his book *Shadow Boxing* (Vision Life Ministries, 1999), Dr. Henry Malone describes many pathways we choose that allow demonic entrances into our lives. Some of these pathways are independence, rebellion and stubbornness along with outright counsel from mediums.

It is easy to see how we open ourselves to evil by our selfish desires to go our own way. Any time we do not trust the Lord and are not aligning ourselves with His plan for our lives, we can easily become independent, stubborn and rebellious. We have to train ourselves not to need to know everything ahead of God's time to reveal it, and instead move forward in faith and confidence in His ability to direct us.

Take a moment to see if you are on the fast track to deception by the enemy. Below, several beliefs and behaviors are listed that can be red flags indicating a demonic hold on your life. Place a check beside any that you seem to struggle with over and over, or that you have had difficulty overcoming.

Anorexia nervosa

Anti-Semitism

Bulimia

Compromise

Confusion

Continuously making
wrong decisions

Cults (false doctrines)

Deception

Doubt

False prophets and
preachers

False teachers

Immaturity

Inappropriate behavior

Intellectualism

Intestinal problems

Irresponsibility

Racism

Sickness

Unbelief

If you checked one or more of these problems, it is possible that your need to know has caused you to move into an area of agreement with the lies of Satan and opened doors to the occult. If you have done so, please do not allow an ungodly fear to continue to torment you. Do not allow a spirit of fear to trouble you. If you feel that God is requiring more faith and trust, be careful that you do not remain in a place of needing to know all the details.

Simply repent of a constant need to know and a lack of trust in God and close the door to demonic attacks. Then draw a bloodline, forbidding the enemy to cross at any time in the future. Begin as Abraham did, stepping out and letting go of your past, and moving forward in trust.

In other words, as we move into a new area we can expect the landscape to change. The promise is the same, but the circumstances surrounding the promise are different. When we fully depend upon God's Spirit, we will not be able to judge by what we see or hear in the natural. "His delight is in the fear of the Lord, and He shall not judge by the sight of His eyes, nor decide by the hearing of His ears" (Isaiah 11:3, nkjv). If we make decisions based on what we see and hear in the natural, we limit God.

Following God requires a greater level of faith. We must develop more mature spiritual senses and spiritual eyesight in order to possess what God has promised us. In order to be on guard and ready, we must learn to depend on the sevenfold Spirit of God. Only by following His direction, using His wisdom and exercising our understanding by the Spirit, will we have success and see the fulfillment of God's promises to us.

### The Dream of the Higher Highway

I remember complaining to the Lord about faith. One night in my prayers before falling asleep, I began to pour out my heart to the Lord: *Father, I can't seem to walk in the faith that Abraham had. I know I am supposed to walk in faith, but trusting You is too difficult. I am the type of person who needs to be able to see where I am going. I have to know the end result. Taking steps before I fully understand is just too hard!* The Lord answered my complaint with a dream.

I dreamed that my husband, Mickey, and I were traveling in a car down a highway. He was driving. There seemed to be fog or mist hindering my view. We were traveling so fast I asked Mickey to slow down. I was terrified. Not only was he driving too fast, but also I could not see where we were going.

After several of my pleas, he finally pulled the car over to the side of the road and stopped on the shoulder. I glanced down and realized we were on a higher level because there was another highway below me. I could see everything down below on the lower highway. But on our higher highway, I could not see ahead.

Then the Lord spoke to me and said that He had placed us on a higher level—a higher way—and that if I really wanted to "see," I could go down to a lower level in the Spirit. If I wanted to remain at this higher level, I would have to trust Him in this new place and develop keener spiritual eyesight. This new level would require greater understanding of the sevenfold Spirit of God.

Praise the Lord that He has promised us His sevenfold Spirit, which empowers us to receive all wisdom and understanding of our times and seasons! We need never to go to any other source but Him to receive all that we need for success in life. I am now fully aware that His blood covenant means that He will never leave me nor forsake me. I can trust Him—and so can you.

## Aligning Our Mission Statement with His

When we align ourselves with Christ's mission statement, then we are fully empowered with every attribute of His Spirit that is needed to fulfill our own tasks. Let's examine His mission and what He was empowered to do:

> The Spirit of the Sovereign LORD is on me, because the LORD has anointed me to preach good news to the poor. He has sent me to bind up the brokenhearted, to proclaim freedom for the captives and release from darkness for the prisoners, to proclaim the year of the LORD's favor and the day of vengeance of our God, to comfort all who mourn, and

provide for those who grieve in Zion—to bestow on them a crown of beauty instead of ashes, the oil of gladness instead of mourning, and a garment of praise instead of a spirit of despair.

Isaiah 61:1–3

We are empowered to fulfill the same mission as Jesus. The Spirit of the Lord, therefore, will anoint us to:

• Preach good news to the poor.
• Bind up the brokenhearted.
• Proclaim freedom for the captives.
• Release the prisoners from darkness.
• Proclaim the year of the Lord's favor.
• Proclaim the day of vengeance of our God.
• Comfort all who mourn.
• Give them a crown of beauty instead of ashes.
• Give them the oil of gladness instead of mourning.
• Give them a garment of praise instead of a spirit of despair.

Dear one, we are crossing over into realms of the supernatural. We are not able to do this mission in our own strength; we need the fullness of the Spirit of the Lord operating within us.

We need the assurance that because we are righteous in Christ we can always run boldly to the throne of grace for a supernatural empowerment to accomplish our mission. We need His divine wisdom, His counsel and direction and the divine knowledge that only He can impart so that we can have victory over the demonic forces that imprison His chosen ones. All of these things are available to each of us as we cross over into a greater level of His glory.

Please pray with me, asking God to empower you with His sevenfold Spirit:

*Father, I come to You submitting to Your divine plan for my life. I realize that I have attempted to control my destiny and possibly have resisted Your plan for my life. I confess that I have sinned, and I repent for opening any doors that allowed the entrance of the occult.*

*I ask that You reveal Your sevenfold Spirit to me. Empower me with Your wisdom, understanding, counsel, might and knowledge. I submit my life to the Spirit of the Lord. You are my God, the God of my life and my future. I will walk in reverential fear of the Lord. I will not judge my circumstances by the natural eye, but I will trust in Your Word. I choose to align my mission with Your mission. In Jesus' name I pray, Amen.*

## Using Your New Heavenly Strategies

You now have several heavenly strategies to fulfill your new mission statement.

- After reading Luke 4:18–20, write down five things that you desire to do for the Lord. Do not focus on religious works—you cannot be righteous through works. Rather focus on your righteousness through the shed blood of Jesus. Allow the Lord to write His mission on your heart. Be sure to write down how you believe the blood of Jesus will empower you.

  1. _____

  2. _____

3. _____

4. _____

5. _____

- Is there someone you know who needs to hear the Gospel? Write down his or her name. Then write down your new strategy as to how you will minister to that person. Plead the blood of Jesus over his/her life and draw a bloodline so that the enemy has to loose his hold from that one.
- Do you have a loved one who is grieving over a death or other loss? Write down the ways in which you could show him or her the love of Christ.

# — 6 —

# RESISTING RELIGIOUS PARADIGMS

And Zacharias said to the angel, "How shall I know this?
For I am an old man, and my wife is well advanced in years."

Luke 1:18, NKJV

I have had so many mind-sets concerning God and what He is saying that He often has to knock me out at night and speak to me in my dreams. That way I cannot argue with Him and dispute what He asks me to do! For people who argue with God—and we all do—dreams and visions are a method of communication God uses to bypass our natural thinking and convey His will and purposes to us.

God used a dream, which I will talk about in a bit, to change my mind concerning my legalistic nature. I have always been a high achiever and a perfectionist. Although I would have told you that I was saved by grace, I innately believed that my righteousness was intact because of "me" and what "I did" for God.

Religion is man's idea of how to worship and serve God. In the Old Testament, God used the Law of Moses as a guideline for His people. The New Testament shows us that Jesus came and fulfilled the Law as He became the sacrifice for our sins. I do not wish to enter into a theological debate. And, this is not a book to dispute what grace is and how grace is abused—meaning "anything is okay because I am under grace." I do, however, want to point out that man has developed numerous strategies, tactics and methods for achieving all types of personal success. But God Himself desires to reveal mysteries that have held us back from achieving success—His way!

Ruling and reigning with Christ begins with the blood and ends with the blood. We will be discovering many strategies as we continue together. Try not to skip ahead to another chapter, as I am attempting to help you lay a solid foundation as you claim your inheritance, both spiritually and naturally. There is a much higher way than relying on your own self-efforts to possess your inheritance in Christ. Dear one, it is all about calling upon Him to save us, cleanse us and empower us to renew our minds concerning His goodness and His desire to bless each of us.

Because of issues of shame in my past, I believed I had to work very hard to receive blessings from God. I figured that my past disqualified me for God's best. Though His grace is a gift (*grace* means "unmerited favor"), I felt as if I had to pray long hours, fast often and quote all the correct Scriptures to convince God to bless me. I knew He died for me, but I did not understand that when He shed His royal blood I was empowered as a daughter (princess) to claim my rightful inheritance—to rule and reign with Christ. Because of the blood of Jesus and His grace, I already had an inheritance!

None of us can earn anything by our own works—it is by grace we are saved and through His grace we are empowered for success in life.

It is important to know this because when we reign in life we reign over sin and powers of darkness. Our inheritance—which we claim now, in this life—involves reigning over powers connected to infirmity, depression and curses. This power to reign is based entirely upon Jesus and only Him.

Read what Romans 5:17 says:

> For if, by the trespass of the one man, death reigned through that one man, how much more will those who receive God's abundant provision of grace and of *the gift of righteousness reign in life through the one man,* Jesus Christ.
>
> (emphasis added)

I thought that to reign in life meant that I had to perform perfectly for God. I know that sounds ridiculous—but I am finding that most of the Church believes the same. There is very little teaching about the cross anymore and even less concerning the blood. I have seen people actually become offended when they hear teaching on the blood of Christ and how good God is. It is almost as if they want to believe God is mean and that He is just waiting to smack His children with a willow stick because they have done something to displease Him. (I know about this because I was one of those people.)

God desires for each of us to receive His grace to live a victorious life. Self-effort will rob us of ruling and reigning. Remember, we cannot save ourselves, heal ourselves or bless ourselves—it all comes from Jesus and the price He paid by shedding His blood.

God wants me to understand the fullness of what Christ did for me. He wants me free from all legalism, rules, regulations and religious perfection. He also wants me to get out of my comfort zone, to resist the religious paradigms with which I was familiar and to follow His will instead of my own. He wants the same for you.

So now let's look at the dream that brought this message home.

## God Opened My Mind

One night after I came home from the church my husband and I pastored, I was so exhausted I went to bed with my Sunday clothes on! I was too tired to undress. I had worked hard to be religious and to prove to everyone around me just how religious I could be.

When I fell asleep, I dreamed that an axe fell from heaven and split my head wide open. Yes, you read that right! Heaven's axe lays open every wrong mind-set and chops that mind-set to the root. It was not a gory dream; there was no blood. God had to get my attention, however, and this dream certainly did that.

As my mind lay wide open, two clothespins fell from heaven, and God's hands used them to pin back my brain on each side. In the natural, clothespins hang clothes out to dry. In my dream I was the one being hung out to dry, in the sense that I was being directed to stay open-minded concerning everything He told me to do.

God said, *Sandie, I am going to clip your mind back so that you have to remain open-minded concerning My truths—especially how you view the blood of Jesus and your strict adherence to legalism and perfectionism in our relationship. If you want to be led by My Spirit, you will have to allow Me to shift you out of your "stinking thinking." Your thought patterns and religious structures are limiting how I want to move through you.*

When I awoke from the dream, I understood the interpretation. I was resisting His grace that had been provided for me by Jesus. I was focusing more on the enemy than the finished work at the cross. Also, I was limiting Him and the way He wanted to move in our church services because the new direction did not fit into my way of doing things. I needed to shift theologically and get out from under the yoke of legalism.

Although Mickey and I felt that we were very open to Him, we both had old belief systems concerning moves of His Spirit and God's goodness. Now God was saying that we must trust Him to anoint us and teach us truths that had been hidden from us. I was to remain open-minded. This was going to require me to let go.

## The Zacharias Lesson

God will use any means necessary to get us out of limited and legalistic thinking. As I stated, He often uses dreams and visions to bypass our minds and plant Holy Spirit computer chips of instruction and wisdom into our brains while we sleep. Most likely God has already been speaking to you concerning changes He wants you to embrace as you move forward by His Spirit.

He also sends angels. Scripture gives us several examples of God sending angels to speak to His children. Remember Zacharias? He knew he was seeing an angel, and argued about the message that the angel, Gabriel, brought from God. Can you imagine having the boldness to argue with Gabriel, who stands in the very presence of God?

For the most part, Zacharias was no different from most of us. He was a conscientious man of God, going about his daily routine. There he was in the Temple, fulfilling his responsibilities, business as usual. I am sure the barrenness he and Elizabeth had experienced was heavy upon his heart, but Scripture does not indicate that Zacharias was doing anything out of the ordinary when Gabriel appeared. He had been selected by lot among the priests to go into the Temple and burn incense, but he was not in an intimate prayer time interceding for his wife and her inability to conceive a child.

But his response to the angel indicates that he was bound by limited thinking. Gabriel appeared and spoke these words: "Do not be afraid, Zacharias, for your prayer is heard; and your wife Elizabeth will bear you a son, and you shall call his name John" (Luke 1:13, NKJV).

Well, this rocked Zacharias's boat! Zacharias was not like Peter, who was eager to walk on water at the bidding of the Lord. Instead of receiving the promise of a son by faith, Zacharias began to argue with Gabriel and explain all the reasons why it was impossible:

> And Zacharias said to the angel, "How shall I know this? For I am an old man, and my wife is well advanced in years." And the angel answered and said to him, "I am Gabriel, who stands in the presence of God, and was sent to speak to you and bring you these glad tidings. But behold, you will be mute and not able to speak until the day these things take place, because you did not believe my words which will be fulfilled in their own time."
>
> Luke 1:18–20, NKJV

Zacharias was experiencing a mind-set problem: He refused to accept the fact that God could and would heal his wife of the curse of barrenness. Surely, he replied, God should consider the difficulties! Elizabeth was not only barren, but now she was too old to have children. After all, having kids at that age was ridiculous! I often wonder what would have been Zacharias's response if he had talked to Abraham and Sarah and met their miracle baby.

As a result of Zacharias's doubt and unbelief in God's ability to make the impossible possible, the angel struck him dumb. Zacharias was unable to speak until his son, John, was born. To ensure that no negative speech would hinder the fruitfulness of the promise, Zacharias would have no verbal input until the time of fulfillment.

What a hard way to learn a hard lesson! I know for a fact that it would almost destroy me if I were unable to talk for nine months. I once had laryngitis and my physician's prescription was for me not to talk for five days. I almost went crazy because I like to talk—I mean, I *really* like to talk! I lasted only three days, and then I caved in and talked up a storm.

But, nonetheless, like Zacharias, I have had to learn the lesson that legalism is not acceptable behavior in God's eyes. In my book *Dream On: Keys to Understanding Dreams and Visions* (Zion Ministries, 2008) I discuss how the Lord sent an angel to speak to my husband when he was in a crisis. I really wanted God to send an angel to speak to me, as well; after all, I was in crisis *with* him!

I remember spending countless hours quoting words and Bible verses demanding a visitation from God. I am sad to admit this, but I became very legalistic with my prayers. This can happen when we believe that we have certain "rights," such as an angelic visitation. I was corrected by the Lord concerning limiting Him. Legalism restricts our ability to hear Him. I then started having dreams of angels visiting me and speaking to me.

When the Lord began to reveal to me that the enemy was disarmed due to the shed blood of Jesus and that it was legalism to quote certain Scriptures over and over, mindlessly, as if speaking a mantra, I had no idea how to respond. Actually, my immediate response was *fear*. I was afraid that if I *changed my routine* and *no longer relied on my religious performance*, the enemy would not just show up for dinner, but come and bring a suitcase!

Believer, when I let go and shifted from "me" and "my faith" to faith in what Jesus had already accomplished I began to feel "free indeed." The "indeed" part of freedom is a measure of freedom that only Christ can supply.

The Bible says that God has "disarmed principalities and powers." We know from Ephesians that these refer to Satan and his cohorts. This was accomplished when Jesus shed His blood at the cross. (Later we will discuss our spiritual weapons and using those weapons to inherit the promise.) It was a hard lesson to learn, but life changing.

## The Children of Israel and Paradigm Shifts

Regarding my three days without talking, actually, that is about the extent of a human's endurance for some of life's challenges. After that, it becomes difficult to remain on track. Whether we face a test of faith, of obedience or of patience and endurance, it is just downright hard to maintain a good attitude and respond properly.

Remember the children of Israel? Only three days after they crossed over the Red Sea, they began to backslide. Three days without water, and they decided that life was too difficult and they could not trust God for their provision. They blamed their problems on Moses and then wanted to go back to Egypt. It is the same for us today. We get "tanked up" on Sunday, and by Wednesday—three days later—we begin to leak!

The problem with the Israelites was that they had a mindset concerning how God spoke to them. In times of transition,

God speaks differently. While they were in Egypt, God spoke to them by promising a deliverer. At their first challenge, they decided that Moses was not capable of leading, so they wanted to elect a new deliverer. Surely, they thought, God would answer their prayers by providing another leader.

God, however, was speaking differently in their transition. God desired to prove Himself to the Israelites by performing a miracle. God had Moses throw a piece of wood into the bitter waters, and the waters were made sweet:

> Then Moses led Israel from the Red Sea and they went into the Desert of Shur. For three days they traveled in the desert without finding water. When they came to Marah, they could not drink its water because it was bitter. (That is why the place is called Marah.) So the people grumbled against Moses, saying, "What are we to drink?"
>
> Then Moses cried out to the LORD, and the LORD showed him a piece of wood. He threw it into the water, and the water became sweet.
>
> There the LORD made a decree and a law for them, and there he tested them.
>
> Exodus 15:22–25

You see, the Israelites had a certain mind-set of how God should speak. They limited Him to the way He had cared for them in the past. The Lord wanted to show Himself as a miracle-working God whom they could trust. God wanted His children to follow Him wholeheartedly and to believe that whatever He promised, He was well able to perform.

Both Zacharias and the camp of Israel were challenged to make a paradigm shift. God wanted to lift them out of old, limiting mind-sets of how He worked in their lives. He was bringing heaven's purposes to the earth in order to bless His children. Remember that while they were in the wilderness and in sin, God reintroduced the blood covenant. Again, God is *never not* pursuing us! He will take us on to that higher road if we respond properly and make a shift into greater faith. God will see that His perfect will is made manifest on earth, if only we will follow Him.

Beloved, God desires to shift us out of old patterns of doubt and unbelief. He wants to deliver us from all our barren situations.

## Paradigms Defined

We have been tossing around this word *paradigm*. But what exactly is a paradigm?

A *paradigm* is a mental structure, a way of thinking. It is a mind-set or model based on human reasoning and behavior. Many times a paradigm is negative. Thus, since a mind-set is by definition rigid and unchanging, a negative paradigm hinders us from believing things can be different. This can damage our faith if we believe we know everything about God and how He works, because we are then prideful. Pride always resists change.

This is the reason so many of us respond negatively when something new comes our way. We are afraid of alterations in our lifestyles and belief systems, preferring familiar beliefs and patterns of behavior. When we cling to a religious paradigm, we do not allow ourselves to think any other way, and we limit God.

Religious structures limit our faith and hope. If God desires to heal someone, for example, we may lock on to the way we believe He should do it, and then we miss how God is telling us to pray for or minister to that person. What if God wanted to heal someone through the skill of a surgeon's hand? If we limit God to the paradigm that He does not use doctors for healing, we might miss His divine plan. If someone has faith that God will perform a miracle, does that mean a miracle will not occur because he has to undergo surgery? Is it not the Lord, *Jehovah-Rapha*, who is the healer, however He performs the healing? You can see how a paradigm might get in the way of the work God wants to do in our lives. Yet these are hard to let go of.

The fifth chapter of John describes a perfect example of someone who was challenged with a paradigm shift. A man who had suffered from a spirit of infirmity for 38 years lay beside the Pool of Bethesda, hoping that someday someone would place him in the waters of healing.

One day Jesus stopped by his side and asked him, "Do you want to get well?" (John 5:6). The man responded with excuses as to why he could not be healed. "The sick man answered Him, 'Sir, I have no man to put me into the pool when the water is stirred up; but while I am coming, another steps down before me'" (verse 7, NKJV). Jesus was ready to heal him at that very instant, but the man was blocked by his negative mind-set. He believed first that he had to wait until an angel came and stirred the waters. Then he believed that he had to be picked up and placed in the water before anyone else got there.

The man's mind-set could have prevented him from receiving the power of Jesus. Jesus was not even going to use the pool as part of the healing. Oh, my! How this exposes our reliance on religion! Jesus replied, "Rise, take up your bed and walk" (verse 8, NKJV). The man changed his mind, and his life: He got up and walked.

How many of us have a mind-set as to how we are going to be made whole? What are we waiting for? Are we bypassing our healing because we believe we need visitations from angels? Do we lose the new job or relationship or financial breakthrough because we expect to see Jesus face to face before His power can transform our lives? Do we miss God's guidance because we want Him to speak in a certain way? In order to walk on the higher way of increased faith, we must not limit God. We need to understand the fact that through the blood covenant we have a legal right to restoration, and then see how God wants to bring it about.

Negative paradigms resist change. Change, therefore, must occur in us for us to make the shift into God's "new thing." Beloved, the new is now! It is time to claim our spiritual inheritance.

## John, Jesus and Paradigm Shifts

The very first book of the New Testament confronts us with a paradigm shift. A new message was being presented through John the Baptist. Maybe you have not seen John the Baptist as a pioneer who introduced a new belief system, but he was.

After Malachi, the last prophet of the Old Testament, the New Testament begins, and it is a radical change. This is a prime example of leaving the old and embracing the new. We are suddenly instructed to embrace a new covenant, a new understanding of our relationship with God. Shifting into Kingdom mentality requires leaving the past behind, getting out of the box and being open-minded to a new way of approaching God.

The voice of John the Baptist in the wilderness introduces us to a new message—the Kingdom message. His theology of repentance challenged everyone, especially the religious leaders, to abandon their religious traditions and to embrace a new lifestyle. He spoke directly to King Herod regarding his sins and to the Jewish religious hierarchy regarding their pride and arrogance. John the Baptist exposed a legalistic religious structure that opposed the Good News of Christ Jesus. John preached that it was not through religious works, family heritage or religious tradition that one would experience the Kingdom of heaven. The Jews were being challenged to receive revelation by the Spirit of God.

This was such a new way of thinking that it completely puzzled the religious leaders. All of their lives the Pharisees, who were particularly legalistic, had studied the Law and prided themselves on their relationship with God through their religious deeds. Why shift out of the old when they had it all figured out?

Jesus challenged the religious system of the Pharisees with the same fortitude as John the Baptist. He added to His daily itinerary many miracles, signs, wonders and deeds that directly opposed their interpretation of the Law. He deliberately healed on the Sabbath, for instance, knowing that the religious structure of His time would resist Him.

Doing God's work on the Sabbath, walking on water, casting out devils and forgiving sins—let me remind you that this did not occur in the Old Testament!—were only a few demonstrations of His credibility as the Son of Man and the Son of God. He shook paradigms of holiness by declaring "clean" what was once called "unclean." He rocked their religious boats by eating with sinners and making disciples of the city's hated tax collectors. He confounded their surefire case against a woman caught in adultery, even though the Law required she be stoned.

As Jesus did the will of His Father, He repeatedly and deliberately challenged the people around Him to think differently. He and John introduced a new way of thinking—a paradigm shift—a new understanding of the Kingdom of God manifested upon the earth.

## Paradigms Close Minds—and Doors

All old paradigms resist new revelation. This means that we will experience some resistance even in our efforts to claim our spiritual inheritances. When the modern prophetic ministry was birthed in the 1980s, it shook the religious system. I was attending the Christian International Conference when the prophetic movement broke forth, and it was one of the most powerful services I have ever attended. Since that time, God has been imparting His insight to many prophetic people, and they are ministering with strong prophetic revelation.

Even though Scripture says we should covet the gift of prophecy (see 1 Corinthians 14:39), many in the Body of Christ expressed opposition to this teaching and ministry. Some church leaders even labeled this movement as heresy and tried to negate the significance of prophetic ministry itself. As the Holy Spirit released His voice through the mouths of prophets, the persecution became more and more intense.

Our Savior faced the same opposition. He obeyed everything His Father asked Him to do. Jesus brought heaven to earth as He did the Father's will upon this planet. Yet the people opposed Him.

Let's be honest. Though it is difficult for many of us to admit this, we resist new moves of the Holy Spirit because of our paradigms. The Holy Spirit is introducing His new wine, a fresh river of power—it is the power based upon the blood of Jesus. For too long in the past we focused on self-righteousness through works, and that mind-set kept us from welcoming any moves of the Holy Spirit. If we refuse to be open-minded, we easily make the same mistakes as the Pharisees and Sadducees who negated the ministry of Christ.

As Jesus taught His disciples to pray, so we are to pray. Our prayer is for the will of the Father to become manifest on this earth—heaven touching earth! The message of the

Kingdom is given by Jesus Christ through His prayer, which is documented in Matthew 6: "This, then, is how you should pray: Our Father in heaven, hallowed be your name, your kingdom come, your will be done on earth as it is in heaven" (verses 9–10).

We cannot trust ourselves in this season when God is pouring out His Spirit on all flesh. We must depend totally upon the voice of the Holy Spirit and see with spiritual eyes, as the Father brings His Kingdom to earth.

Resisting paradigms requires radical behavior! This does not imply that one should be unstable or "weird." But it does mean that in order to reframe an old paradigm, we must be brave, bold and adamant in servanthood for the Lord. And rather than throw away accountability with our new radical behavior, we should become even more accountable and submitted to godly authority and to God's Word.

Jesus was radical and was labeled a heretic and false prophet. He was a revolutionary who led a revolution. He introduced a new paradigm wherever He taught. He was persecuted and rejected—and that very same persecution might also happen to each of us. But I would rather follow Him than pursue a religious structure that shuts Him out.

## Releasing Control

After my dream of God laying the axe to the root of my religious spirit, things changed in our church. When my husband and I began to back away from the way we thought God wanted to move and instead allowed Him to move the way He wanted, we began to see tremendous breakthrough.

At first it was difficult to let go of our control. Although we did not view ourselves as controlling, we were. We feared that letting go would give those whom we pastored a license to get weird and flaky. But even more than that, we feared doing something wrong. Mickey and I never want to lead a congregation in a wrong direction. We want to provide a place of safety and refuge. Opening our services to something new meant we had to become more vulnerable, and we felt a sincere responsibility to protect the sheep over whom God had given us charge.

Here is an example. I remember well when Spirit-led laughter came into our church. The release of joy and laughter was wonderful and refreshing, but I still struggled with mind-sets concerning this new wine.

I knew it was a divine move of God's Spirit, but I remember feeling out of control and being concerned about how others might view it. Unfortunately, this "new thing" of God was misunderstood and labeled as flaky. Some members of our congregation actually left the church because the way God was moving did not fit their religious paradigms. It would have been easier to embrace a new move of the Holy Spirit if we had not had to contend with the religious spirits that came immediately to discredit us and our integrity.

But it was worth it. When we backed off and trusted the Holy Spirit to direct us through each service, it was always powerful! We had tapped in to a river of anointing that we had never experienced before. We witnessed signs and wonders, healings and a new level of prophetic ministry. At times we were unable to preach because His presence was so strong, so we simply ministered healing, prophecy and deliverance as directed by His Spirit. Sometimes we could not walk to the pulpit without falling flat on our faces—as happened to me in the experience I wrote about in chapter 4. We began to trust that He is always in control, and as a result we gradually let go of our fear that people will get weird or strange, or try to take over the service.

In my flesh I have sweated my way through this new experience. My spirit, however, abounds. Every time I attempt to take back control, I quench the anointing. I have learned to trust Him, to back away from my negative paradigms and to allow His Holy Spirit to move and minister. There is always proper order—including submission to authority—as we maintain reverence for the Holy Spirit.

If I were to pick one of God's sevenfold attributes to describe this, I would say that we are embracing the fear of the Lord. We have become so careful not to grieve the Holy Spirit that we always prefer His way over our own way.

## Even the Patriarchs Had Paradigms

When a person has a religious paradigm—a mind-set or limited way of thinking—it is quite obvious. We see it revealed in his or her responses to God's Word. If, for example, God gives a prophetic word to someone that she can be healed, the person with a religious mind-set might respond, "But the doctor said I have only a few months to live!" Or if a person receives a prophecy that declares, "You are going to buy a new car," his negative paradigm will say, "But I can't even pay my rent!"

This is nothing new. Even the biblical patriarchs had paradigms. We already discussed Zacharias. Abraham presents another example of limited thinking. In a vision God told him, "Your reward will be great!" Abraham's mind-set spoke, "But I am childless" (see Genesis 15:1–2). Sarah had the same mind-set; they both laughed at the prophecy of a son. And yet, even though Abraham had some problems, God still considered him "righteous"! And, let me remind you that it was Abraham with whom God made covenant—the covenant we share as his seed.

And, what about Gideon? From the very beginning, we notice Gideon's negative paradigm concerning the Lord's promise to protect the Israelites. Once while he was threshing his grain in hiding, fearful that the enemy Midianites would steal it, an angel appeared and said to him, "God is with you!" Gideon shook his head and said, "How can God be with us? And by the way, where are the miracles?" (see Judges 6:13). Years of oppression by a powerful enemy had framed his thinking into a negative mind-set. Gideon obviously had a poverty mentality and could not trust God for his safety and provision.

## Tearing Down Idols

Just like the biblical patriarchs—and matriarchs, too—we struggle with old belief systems. Many of us have suffered lack, sickness, oppression and hopelessness, and our paradigms follow those realities instead of faith in God's power. In order to break free from those entrenched negative paradigms that hinder our faith, we must shift into a new belief system. We must begin to believe the Word of God and trust in the God of our breakthrough.

Let's look at Gideon once more. He did not just have a false belief system concerning God; his paradigms concerning himself were also exposed. God called to him, "Gideon, mighty man of valor!" Gideon's belief system—his paradigm—spoke up and said, "I am the very least among my people!" (See Judges 6:15.)

Many of us respond the same as Gideon. When God speaks into our destiny, our response is, "Who, me? But, God, don't You know I don't speak so well? I'm not old enough. I haven't been to seminary. I didn't do well in school."

Some of my paradigms have sounded like this:

"God, I don't have time to take on more responsibility." (I did not understand how to have faith for the grace of God to fulfill all that He asked me to do.)

"God, I don't have the energy to do what You are requiring." (Again, not understanding how to have grace for more faith.)

"God, I am not certain I am able to pastor a church." (Shall I mention grace once more?)

"God, I can't speak well." (Yep, I could not receive grace. It is all about "me.")

"God, how can I deal with one more challenge?" (Well, if I understood God's grace, I could accept the challenge . . . with courage!)

"God, You want me to do *what*?" (Not perceiving grace left me feeling empty, and an empty well leaves one feeling dry.)

"Who, *me*?" (Obviously it was always a "me" problem with little focus on the finished work of Christ.)

It has taken quite a while to get to the victory side of some of these paradigms, and I am still working on the others. But looking back, I am so grateful God overlooked my doubt and unbelief. He kept calling forth my untapped potential until I finally aligned myself with the truth of what He spoke. And now that I understand the power that we have because of the blood of Jesus, I expect complete fulfillment as I lay claim to every promise God has given to me. I have learned how to receive grace from God for every spiritual assignment—what a wonderful shift!

Though we may find ourselves in spiritual battles or experiencing persecution, the victory is ours because of the finished work of Christ. There will be a season when God will confront your paradigms. You will be challenged to come forth with all that God sees in you. He will speak to your potential and then expect you to let go of any old paradigms that limit you from fulfilling your destiny.

Gideon's primary assignment is a reflection of our own starting place: to destroy the idols that were in his own backyard. Before he was fully empowered to lead the Israelites into battle, he first had to destroy the idols of his ancestors.

We have to remember how much God hates idolatry. Both the Old and New Testaments address the sin of idolatry. Worshiping idols is not limited to bowing down to a statue of Buddha or other graven image. If we exalt the enemy's words above God's words, then we are committing idolatry.

God and His Word are one; they cannot be separated from each other. If we honor Satan's words about us—words such as *useless, unable to succeed, hopeless, a failure, rejected, abandoned* and *shameful*—above what God has said—that we are *the head and not the tail, blessed, healed, delivered, successful, anointed, loved* and *accepted*—then we are committing idolatry! If we believe the lies of the devil, then it is time to re-landscape our backyards, as Gideon did. As we tear down false belief systems, we also are tearing down old structures that have dominated our thinking.

And guess what Gideon did when the angel appeared to him? You guessed it, I am certain. He built an altar! Yes, an altar for a blood sacrifice and worship. Gideon was baptizing his land of promise, so to speak. Gideon was starting to understand. He called that place "The Lord Is Peace." How awesome is that? Peace came into Gideon's heart once God revealed his destiny and purpose. All along, Gideon was being empowered to claim his future.

As I stated before, paradigms resist change. So in order to move forward, God requires that we make paradigm shifts. This means renewing our minds by tearing down false idols and fully accepting God's Word concerning us.

Tearing down paradigms and reestablishing God's truth is a spiritual battle. But oh! is it worth the time and effort when we move into that new and awesome place of victory.

## Four Requirements for a New Paradigm

Are you ready to shift into a new level of His glory? Are you excited about heaven touching earth? Are you even more excited to claim your inheritance?

Four things are required in order to make this giant leap into God's new thing:

1. Allow God to intervene at any time He desires.
2. Allow God to change your vision.
3. Allow God to expand your vision continually and empower you to move from glory to greater levels of glory.
4. Keep your focus on the victory we have due to the blood.

First, we must always allow God to intervene in our thoughts and our actions—especially within our ministry times. When I was a pastor (God has led Mickey and me into a new ministry, as I will mention in a moment), I really believed I did this—until the Lord challenged me with an old paradigm. It was not that I had a problem with the particular move of His Spirit; the problem was with the persecution that occurred as a result of His moving.

When persecution comes because you have allowed the Holy Spirit the freedom to minister, you will be tempted to stop. Do not stop, and do not look back. The solution to persecution is not to run but to embrace the fireball. Become addicted to radical passion, and you will make it across to the other side of your test. Once I understood the freedom that is promised due to God's grace and the power of the blood, I no longer attempted to perform for others when I ministered. I cannot begin to explain the pressure I used to feel when I ministered the Word. Now, I just rely on Him—it is so wonderful!

Second, allow God to change or expand your vision. A vision can become a negative paradigm itself. Think about this for a moment. We often believe that we must never allow the original vision God gives us to change. A church congregation, for instance, might print the vision statement in the bulletin and keep it at the forefront of community life and ministry. Emphasis is placed on catching the vision.

A vision, however, is not etched in stone like the Ten Commandments! Most likely our visions will expand as the Holy Spirit moves upon us. If we have a religious paradigm in place, though, we might have trouble with this. We will want to hang on to the original vision, the familiar old way, to ensure that it is fulfilled.

As congregations and individuals, we must ask ourselves this question: *Did God really give me that original vision, or was it partly my own desire?* You see, most of the time our own personal desires are expressed in a vision. This is not a bad thing—as long as we allow the Lord to purify it. As a result, it becomes fully His vision. Remember this one statement: *It is not about us; it is all about Him.*

Third, when God expands the vision, allow Him to keep expanding. Resist locking into another paradigm after the first major shift has taken place. Keep moving and shifting. Scripture says that we move from faith to faith, strength to strength and glory to glory: "But we all, with unveiled face, beholding as in a mirror the glory of the Lord, are being transformed into the same image from glory to glory, just as by the Spirit of the Lord" (2 Corinthians 3:18, NKJV). This means that He will challenge us with new levels of faith and give us strength for every new level. This will empower us to embrace glory, more glory and even greater levels of His glory.

Fourth, keep your focus on the victory we have through the blood. Chapters 1 and 2 concern the power of the blood and blood covenant. Why not thumb through those chapters, take some new notes and apply the revelation right now? In fact, list a few areas concerning the power of the blood that have empowered you:

1. _____

2. _____

3. _____

4. _____

5. _____

## Points to Consider

Let's commit now to move from our old paradigms, embrace God's new thing for us and move from glory to glory. Here are eight points to consider.

1. God speaks differently during transition. Be careful not to limit His direction based on how He spoke in the past.
2. In times of transition, it is more beneficial to embrace a new level of faith rather than to speak quickly against new direction. Remember, God had to shut the mouth of Zacharias so that the Word of the Lord would be fulfilled.

3. Be on guard and protect each infilling of His power. Remember, the children of Israel got filled up with great faith, but by the third day, they began to leak.
4. A religious paradigm is a mental structure that limits us from growing in God's grace. Take care not to allow any structure that opposes God's "new thing" to remain in position.
5. If you are feeling pressure from the paradigm shift, you are in good company: The patriarchs of old are in your winner's circle!
6. Radical behavior is required during these radical seasons of change.
7. It is not about us; it is all about Him.
8. Have faith in the grace of God to empower you to claim your full inheritance.

# — 7 —

# EVERY KNEE MUST BOW

That in (at) *the name of Jesus* every knee should (must) bow,
in heaven and on earth and under the earth, and every tongue
[frankly and openly] confess and acknowledge that Jesus
Christ is Lord, to the glory of God the Father.

Philippians 2:10–11, AMPLIFIED (emphasis added)

Unlike most of us, who might or might not have a nick-
name, God has many different names. To help us grasp
the fact that God wants us to walk into our inheritances,
let's discover what He reveals about Himself through some
of these names. Understanding His character as it is defined
in this way is pivotal to our times of transition: His names
reveal His leading and provision for us on our journey to
our inheritances.

We will examine the name *Jesus* in a moment, but keep
in mind that Philippians 2:9–10 says that this is "the name
that is above every name, that in (at) the name of Jesus every

knee should (must) bow" (AMPLIFIED). This means that as
we begin to possess our royal inheritance, we hold high the
name of Jesus.

## God's Various Names

When Scripture refers to a *name of God*, the Hebrew word
*shem* is used, which implies what someone is famous for. Is
that not an awesome thought? The names of God tell us what
He is famous, or known, for. All the names of God are the
attributes of what He has done and is still able to do for us.
The names of God imply His reputation, His glory (what He
receives glory for being and doing) and His fame.

The word *name* is derived from another Hebrew word,
*suwm*, which implies that through a name something is established. Each time God revealed an attribute of His fame,
reputation and glory to His people, He revealed a new name.
By revealing His name, He set things in divine order so that
the attributes of His name could be accomplished. In other
words, through God's many different names, He brings divine
order to our circumstances by releasing or establishing the
attributes each name implies.

The first verse in the Bible gives us the most frequently used
name for God in Scripture: *Elohim*, the "Creator God." It
also suggests "the strong One" and "the three in One." The
familiar opening verse reads, "In the beginning God created
the heavens and the earth" (Genesis 1:1).

Then comes *El Elyon*, "God Most High," a name spoken
by Melchizedek, king of Salem and priest of God, who blessed
Abraham: "Blessed be Abram by God Most High, Creator
of heaven and earth. And blessed be God Most High, who
delivered your [Abraham's] enemies into your hand" (Genesis
14:19–20). This expresses God's sovereignty.

Genesis 22 tells how God tested Abraham's willingness to sacrifice his son Isaac and after the test provided the sacrificial offering. Abraham called that place *Jehovah-Jireh*, meaning "the Lord will provide" (see Genesis 22:14). This was a shadow of the blood sacrifice that Jesus would later offer for our divine provision.

Up until the time God commissioned Moses, the Israelites knew God predominately by one name: *El-Shaddai*, "God Almighty" (see Exodus 6:3), which, among other translations, can be rendered "the many-breasted One" and represents the mothering nature of God. The name reminds us of a mother bear who viciously fights any predator that intends to harm her young. In *El-Shaddai*, we recognize One who "mothered" the Israelites—fed, nurtured and protected them.

When Moses approached Pharaoh, telling him to release God's people, the Israelites' troubles only increased. Moses pled with God to rescue His people and, in answer, God revealed His personal name: "Lord." This is represented in Hebrew by the four consonants *YHWH*, and rendered in English as *Jehovah*.

> And God spake unto Moses, and said unto him, I am the Lord: and I appeared unto Abraham, unto Isaac, and unto Jacob, by the name of God Almighty, but by my name Je-hovah was I not known to them. And I have also established my covenant with them, to give them the land of Canaan, the land of their pilgrimage, wherein they were strangers.
>
> Exodus 6:2–4, KJV

This is very exciting because the name *Jehovah* speaks of the God of our future. He was introducing Himself as "the all-existing One," "God who is and was and is evermore to be." The Israelites had never embraced Him as Lord. It was time for them to be released from their bondage and cross over into their place of promise. God was revealing Himself as the One who was in the beginning and knows the end.

After the Israelites miraculously crossed the Red Sea and began traversing the desert, God answered their cries for water and revealed Himself as *Jehovah-Rapha*, "the LORD who heals us" (see Exodus 15:26).

His identity as healer foreshadows Jesus' atoning death. We read in Numbers 21:9 that Moses was instructed to lift up on a pole a bronze replica of a serpent. Any Israelite who was bitten by a venomous snake could look up at the image and live. He was revealing His desire to save mankind: "And just as Moses lifted up the serpent in the desert [on a pole], so must [so it is necessary that] the Son of Man be lifted up [on the cross]" (John 3:14, AMPLIFIED).

You can see from this sampling that God is able to establish for us all that His names declare—not only for our salvation, but also for our daily needs. This is an awesome revelation. Thus, if we are struggling with finances, we know that He is *Jehovah-Jireh*, "the LORD our provider," and that He will supply all our needs (see Genesis 22:14). Our only responsibility is to receive that attribute with faith in His name and believe that He is able to provide.

Likewise, *Jehovah-Shalom* means He is "the LORD of peace" (see Judges 6:24). Jesus said that it is He who gives peace, not peace that the world gives, but peace that comes only from Him. Our eternal peace is assured as we are forgiven, sanctified, justified and cleansed by the blood of Jesus (see John 14:27).

Knowing God's names and knowing that He desires to bless us with His attributes empowers us to move forward and fulfill our divine destinies. Remember: He is Lord! He knows our future and is able to accomplish what He has promised. "'Behold, the days are coming,' says the LORD, 'that I will perform that good thing which I have promised to the house of Israel and to the house of Judah'" (Jeremiah 33:14, NKJV).

If we are honest with ourselves, though, we will admit that we, like the Israelites, limit God and His ability to accomplish what He has promised. We do not bow before Him in homage, but rather doubt that He is who He says He is. This is why we fail to receive God's best for our lives. It is the very mind-set we are changing, as we journey on to embrace our inheritances.

## The Name of Jesus

Let's fast-forward now to the New Testament and look at the name of Jesus, second Person of the Holy Trinity. I mentioned earlier that Christ, the sacrificial Lamb, was slain before the foundation of the world (see 1 Peter 1:19–21). This means that before Creation sprang into being through God's spoken Word, He had a "backup plan" to redeem mankind from sin. Sin requires punishment and God loves us so much that He chose to become our sacrifice, a sacrificial Lamb that would cover our sin and redeem us from our punishment required for that sin.

Jesus came. Wow! I could stop there—in fact, it is difficult to catch my breath after writing that down. Just to imagine how He came, why He came and what He suffered *because* He came tenders my heart once again.

Just as we did with the Old Testament names for God, when studying a New Testament name, we need to look at the character and work of the person to understand its significance. Matthew 1:21 tells us this: "Thou shalt call his name JESUS; for he shall save his people from their sins" (KJV). The name *Jesus* is of Hebrew origin: *Yehowshuwa* or *Yehowshu'a* (both pronounced as yeh-ho-*shoo*-ah).

Allow me to cut to the chase and just say it plainly: Jesus is the Savior, the One who saves us from sin and the eternal separation from God it brought about. We are "saved" in the name of Jesus (Acts 4:12; Romans 10:13), "justified in the name of the Lord Jesus Christ" (1 Corinthians 6:11) and forgiven "through his name" (Acts 10:43).

In the New Testament account of Saul's conversion, we read that men and women "called upon the name" of Jesus (Acts 9:14, 21). When we "name the name" of Christ (confess His name), we are in essence calling on His name, acknowledging that we belong to Him and that we accept Him as Lord of our lives (see 2 Timothy 2:19).

It goes on. The "name of Jesus" represents the authority and power with which He was mantled, such as working miracles and casting out evil spirits. We are told to baptize "in" or "into" the name of Jesus Christ (Acts 2:38; 22:16), to gather together in His name, to acknowledge Him and, ultimately, "whatever you do, whether in word or deed, do it all in the name of the Lord Jesus" (Colossians 3:17). Simply praying "in the name of Jesus" releases supernatural power and authority to shift atmospheres, change cultures and bring forth the miraculous.

I am reminded how Noah baptized the land with a blood sacrifice when he left the ark. When we are baptized in the name of Jesus, our "land" (meaning both our promised land and ourselves—we were fashioned from dust, right?) is covered with His precious blood.

Believer, listen up again—this is important: *Let us now begin to baptize our promises from God with the blood of Christ.* Your promised land awaits your applying the blood. What promises has God given you? Take some time and examine your promised inheritance. Declare that the blood of Jesus covers that ground. As you pray, remember to pray in the name of Jesus.

Look at a few more examples of what happens when we pray in His name and minister in His name:

- "I will do whatever you ask in my name, so that the Son may bring glory to the Father" (John 14:13).
- "Until now you have not asked for anything in my name. Ask and you will receive, and your joy will be complete" (John 16:24).
- "And these attesting signs will accompany those who believe: in My name they will drive out demons; they will speak in new languages; they will pick up serpents; and [even] if they drink anything deadly, it will not hurt them; they will lay their hands on the sick, and they will get well" (Mark 16:17–18, AMPLIFIED).
- "And I will do [I Myself will grant] whatever you ask in My Name [as presenting all that I AM], so that the Father may be glorified and extolled in (through) the Son. [Yes] I will grant [I Myself will do for you] whatever you shall ask in My Name [as presenting all that I AM]" (John 14:13–14, AMPLIFIED).

Life is about transition. We cannot move forward into our inheritances until we are willing to believe that God is all that He says He is and that He will do all that He says He will do. Using Jesus' mighty name automatically grants us not only redemption but victory in possessing our royal inheritance.

## Leap into Your Future!

I have to say that I was slow to grasp this. For starters I was nervous when it came time to leave home. Well, let me clarify that. My parents had to kick me out of the nest because I had become dependent on their protection, their insight—and their money!

As a college student, I enjoyed the carefree dormitory lifestyle because my tuition and housing were provided by my parents. One summer I decided to pursue summer employment. I moved into an apartment and found a minimum-wage job. Needless to say, it was a hungry summer. I lasted three months in the work force and then went back to college for the easy life.

When it came time to leave home permanently, I was terribly afraid. I was getting married and insecurity regarding my future tormented me. *What if we don't have enough money? What if I can't find a decent job?* These thoughts troubled me for days before our wedding. Finally my mother sat me down and said, "Sandie, you have to leave now!"

When it is time for us to step out and leave "home"—our secure place—we have to trust the LORD (*Jehovah*), the God of our future. We have to bow before the mighty name of Jesus and believe that God will be our Comforter and Protector as we journey. We have to move forward.

A mother eagle prepares her eaglets to leave their nest by removing pieces of soft down a little at a time. Over a period of a few days the soft down is removed and all that is left is a nest full of sharp twigs and thorns. The eaglets have little choice but to leave that prickly nest and fly away.

It is the same with each of us when God prepares us to take a leap of faith out of a familiar place. We become dissatisfied. We are dry and thirsty and realize we need change. God has caused our place of comfort to become uncomfortable, and we have no choice but to leave the nest. This is when the LORD, the God of our future, takes over.

## The Vision of His Fireball

Shortly after Mickey and I stopped pastoring a local church and embraced our new responsibilities as traveling ministers,

God began preparing us to meet Him in a new way. He began to speak to us concerning a Kingdom Training Center.

Suddenly we were being challenged to embrace yet another transition. We would no longer be pastors or ministers; we would oversee a training center apostolically. Although this was a different concept of training, we knew God was speaking to us concerning this new venture.

At first my negative paradigms arose: *God, what do You mean build a Kingdom Training Center? What is a Kingdom Training Center? Whatever it is, we simply cannot do it!*

Then I had a vision that helped me make the shift into this portion of our inheritance. I saw a fireball hurtling toward me. I knew the fireball was from heaven. As it came closer, the Lord said, *Keep what I have just spoken holy. Separate what I have just spoken and keep it holy before Me. Do not allow it to become defiled with doubt and unbelief, but place it firmly in your heart. Do not allow the enemy to steal it from you, but keep it holy before Me.*

I knew God wanted me to take very seriously what He had just spoken about the concept of a Kingdom Training Center. With fear and trembling, I jumped up and ran to find pen and paper to write down the vision. Within a few minutes, I found myself in the Scriptures, turning to the story of the burning bush. I knew that God had revealed His name to Moses in a call to holiness, and I wanted to learn all I could from that example.

## Keeping It Holy

When Moses met God at the burning bush, on the far side of the desert on the mountain of God (see Exodus 3:1), the first thing God said was for Moses to take off his sandals, for the ground on which he was standing was holy. Actually, not one molecule of the mountain had changed, but because God revealed His character of holiness there, it became holy.

But it was more than simply the dirt that was holy: God was also addressing the ground of Moses' heart. What God was speaking into Moses' heart was holy, and Moses was instructed to separate it from what he thought about himself, to realize his potential and to embrace the holiness of God's will over his life. Every time Moses doubted his call, he could remember this revelation and keep holy what God had said.

When we are shifting into our own promised lands, the thief attempts to steal our destiny. We must guard against this. How? Every time God speaks to us, we must treat the ground as holy. We must respond as if He is revealing a new name. Even if we feel inadequate, we must believe that He is well able to show us the particular aspect of His character that will help us enter our land of inheritance.

Can you imagine how worn out Moses was toward the end of his wilderness journey? I suppose he had to protect his heart every time he was challenged in the wilderness with the murmuring Israelites. "Keeping it holy" through the dry seasons is difficult, especially when the devil is tempting you to throw in the towel.

But failing to honor His character—as revealed in His name—in those hard times can have dreadful results. When the Israelites needed another drink of water, their incessant complaining finally pushed Moses over the edge, and he struck a rock in order to produce water. He failed to keep God's instructions holy and separate, and let his emotions take over. This act of disobedience cancelled his crossing over into his promise.

No matter how difficult it may be, separate yourself from your emotions during a season of transition. Emotions are connected to past circumstances, frustrations and fears. Keep holy what God has told you. Ask Him to reveal Himself to you in new ways.

Our role is to use the heavenly strategies He has given us:

1. Remember that God does not sound the same when you are in transition.
2. Remember to keep what God says to you "holy" during this time of transition.
3. Remember that the God of your future desires to reveal Himself to you.

Trust His Word. Listen to His voice. Keep what He says holy. And get ready to meet Him in a new way.

## Thoughts to Consider

- Consider the names of God discussed in this chapter, and think how He has revealed Himself to you in that manner.

---

---

---

- Has the Lord spoken something "different" to you? In other words, are you in the middle of a transition? Then, most likely, you are going to be required to "keep it holy." List below how you do this.

---

---

---

- Is God revealing Himself to you as the God of your future? What prophetic words have you received that involve the new? List below your plans for the future and how you are determined to make the shift.

  _____

  _____

  _____

- Name the "fireball" that you must embrace as you move into your future. Then, write a prayer to the Lord asking for His divine grace.

  _____

  _____

  _____

# — 8 —

# COMING OUT OF THE
# WILDERNESS

And for about forty years like a *fatherly nurse* He cared for
them in the wilderness and endured their behavior.

Acts 13:18, AMPLIFIED (emphasis added)

No one asks for a wilderness experience. We do not pray
to God to send us away into a place where we no longer
sense close fellowship and communion with Him. Yet it is
not uncommon to find ourselves precisely there.

The book of Exodus describes the wilderness, where the
children of Israel wandered for forty years, as a desolate, disor-
derly and lonely place. It was dry, wild, unfruitful and barren.

Can you relate to these descriptions? Do you sometimes
feel lonely, barren and unfruitful? Have you been so dry and
thirsty that you found yourself crying out to God in despera-
tion? Is your life in disorder? Are you at times confused and

irritated? Have you responded to your circumstances with *wild* behavior while in your *wild*erness?

If you can relate, then read on. Certainly God has a purpose for your wilderness: It is the doorway to your inheritance. I love the opening Scripture for this chapter, Acts 13:18 in the Amplified version, which describes God as a "fatherly nurse" who cared for His children while in the wilderness. It relates to the Old Testament prophecy concerning the coming Messiah in Isaiah 61:1–3, and how He would heal those who are broken, proclaim liberty and offer comfort to those who mourn.

What an incredible example of a "fatherly nurse" is represented in His Son, who came to care for all who call on His name! Read below the prophecy recorded by Isaiah:

> The Spirit of the Lord GOD is upon me; because the LORD hath anointed me to preach good tidings unto the meek; he hath sent me to bind up the brokenhearted, to proclaim liberty to the captives, and the opening of the prison to them that are bound; to proclaim the acceptable year of the LORD, and the day of vengeance of our God; to comfort all that mourn; to appoint unto them that mourn in Zion, to give unto them beauty for ashes, the oil of joy for mourning, the garment of praise for the spirit of heaviness; that they might be called trees of righteousness, the planting of the LORD, that he might be glorified.
>
> Isaiah 61:1–3, KJV

Now read what Jesus said concerning His mission. Keep in mind that as He stood in the synagogue to declare why He came, He knew that to fulfill His mission His blood had to be shed for our sakes. In other words, His blood guaranteed that we would possess everything intended for our royal inheritance:

> The Spirit of the Lord [is] upon Me, because He has anointed Me [the Anointed One, the Messiah] to preach the good news (the Gospel) to the poor; He has sent Me to announce release

to the captives and recovery of sight to the blind, to send forth as delivered those who are oppressed [who are downtrodden, bruised, crushed, and broken down by calamity], to proclaim the accepted and acceptable year of the Lord [the day when salvation and the free favors of God profusely abound].

Luke 4:18–19, AMPLIFIED

## The Wilderness

A wilderness is a dry place—no doubt about that. Someone without a job may feel he or she is experiencing a wilderness. Someone without a mate may consider loneliness a wilderness experience. Wildernesses are defined according to many different circumstances. But the Good News is this: Christ has shed His blood to equip us to come out of that wilderness.

I know it will challenge someone's theology when I say that many times it is God who sends us into a dry, desolate place. Although there are seasons when Satan attempts to cover us with darkness and lead us into desolation and hopelessness, we cannot automatically blame a wilderness experience on the devil. After all, Jesus was led by the Spirit to His wilderness to be tempted by Satan (see Luke 4). It was not the devil who led Him; it was God who led Jesus to the dry place. Why? Jesus' victory over the demonic temptations helped empower Him for the miraculous. It strengthened Him and helped prepare Him for the road to the cross.

The word *tempted* is translated as "to try, to prove and to examine." It also implies that Jesus was actually on trial to prove what He believed. He was tested to prove His character and steadfastness. In His desert experience, Jesus grew even stronger in His faith, and gave the devil a black eye at the same time.

It is the same with us. When we go through wilderness times, our faith and character are tested. In these times of testing we learn whether or not our hearts are filled with faith or with doubt and unbelief. We also learn about our hidden selfish motives and attitudes. These things need to be exposed and addressed.

Know this for certain: If we understand the power of the blood, we will come through each wilderness experience and be stronger for having done so.

## The "Proceeding Word"

While He was in the wilderness, Jesus used what I refer to as a "proceeding word." A proceeding word is any Word of God that is proclaimed to the enemy when we are tempted to come into agreement with evil. An example of a proceeding word is Jesus' proclamation to Satan, quoting from the book of Deuteronomy: "It is written, 'Man shall not live on bread alone, but on every word that proceeds out of the mouth of God'" (Matthew 4:4, NASB).

Proceeding words are God-given declarations based on the Word of God that flow from our innermost being. Like a mighty river, God's Word should gush forth from our mouths whenever we are in a wilderness and the enemy is tempting us. God is seeking people who allow themselves to be developed in the wilderness so that they become empowered with these proceeding words.

Rather than feeling sorry for ourselves because we experience dry places, we must realize that God has a greater plan. He is empowering us for the "greater things" that Jesus spoke about.

Most prophets are indicating that the Church is entering into a season of apostolic signs and wonders. In order for us to believe and receive miracles for ourselves and others, we must develop a proceeding word. We must know and understand the Word of God.

In addition, we must rid ourselves of religious mind-sets concerning the miraculous. We must flow with His Spirit and allow Him to move when He desires. Timing is crucial when following the Holy Spirit. He moves in His own timing, and we must develop spiritual sensitivity if we are going to embrace His Kingdom message.

## Tests for Promotion

In my own life, I have observed many wilderness experiences whenever God was planning to move me to a higher spiritual level. During these times I have felt as if I am going through a dark tunnel—I cannot see clearly. I am spiritually dry and, therefore, crying out for a breakthrough. In other words, I get desperate for God.

In the midst of all of this, God is watching and listening to all of my responses. He is testing my heart, my motives. When He shows me that I do not have godly responses, I repent. I begin to come out of the wilderness when I firmly develop that "proceeding word" and take my stand in the power of the blood. Many, many times I have taken Communion during these wilderness experiences, reminding the devil that Christ shed His blood so that I can be made whole. In other words, my response to the devil is to quote the Word of God and my prophetic promises. To my amazement, although I feel I do not deserve it, God brings me through. (Thank God for His amazing grace!)

Once I am out of the wilderness and flowing again in the Spirit, I look back and thank the Lord for the lesson in spiritual maturity. This is what I commonly refer to as "promotion in the Spirit."

I believe the Church is in a season in which God is testing our hearts, motives and responses because He desires to promote us. Whenever we desire to grow, have a more effective ministry and extend the Kingdom of God, we face tests of promotion. It is as if we are students in the "School of the Holy Spirit." A test of promotion is one of the most difficult tests to pass.

But once we pass it and are on the other side of the test, we look back and see that we have been promoted. We have arrived at a higher spiritual level. When Jesus endured forty days of fasting and the difficult temptations He faced, He came out of His wilderness experience in victory with power and might. This is God's goal for us, as well—that we leave our wildernesses in victory, moving in the power and might of His Spirit and doing greater works for His Kingdom than we were doing before.

If you are in the wilderness, God wants to bring you out to higher ground. The way to come out is to realize that God is waiting for you to speak a proceeding word. Give it! He wants to promote you and use you in a mighty way.

But make sure you are ready for it. You might come out for a while and then find yourself back in another test. If so, just begin to speak another proceeding word. While we are in the wilderness, we need to grow and mature and have His Word so impregnated in our spirits that we come forth in power and might.

In the wilderness, begin to speak what God says about you. Remember all your prophetic promises and proclaim them. At every test, use a proceeding word to break out of your captivity. A slave mentality says that God will not fulfill His Word; the proceeding word says that He promises to perform His Word. The proceeding word says that God has firmly planted you into your destiny, and you will not be plucked out of it.

Recognize every ungodly belief and replace it with God's Word. Then stand in the power of the blood. You will experience your deliverance. When you begin to respond to every wilderness test with a proceeding word spoken in faith, you will achieve your destiny.

## Cutting the Umbilical Cord to the Past

Leaving the wilderness and crossing over into our place of destiny requires action on our part. Yes, Jesus shed His precious blood for our freedom, deliverance and healing. But we must make a firm decision to cut the cords to the past so that we can embrace all that He won for us at the cross.

When the Israelites were set free from Pharaoh and the bondage of Egypt, they were cut loose from the only life they had ever experienced. They walked away from it physically, but their belief systems went with them. Thus, they were unable to let go completely of the past.

In Ezekiel 16 we find an allegory that God spoke to His people through the prophet. It gives the picture of an umbilical cord that had held Israel in bondage for generations:

> "Son of man, cause Jerusalem to know her abominations, and say, 'Thus says the Lord God to Jerusalem: "Your birth and your nativity are from the land of Canaan; your father was an Amorite and your mother a Hittite. As for your nativity, on the day you were born your navel cord was not cut, nor were you washed in water to cleanse you; you were not rubbed with salt nor wrapped in swaddling cloths. No eye pitied you, to do any of these things for you, to have compassion on you; but you were thrown out into the open field, when you yourself were loathed on the day you were born."'"
>
> Ezekiel 16:2–5, NKJV

In the natural, an umbilical cord is necessary for providing nourishment and oxygen to a baby in the womb. After the child is born, the cord is meant to be cut. The connection to the old system of life, if you will, must be severed so that the child can grow properly.

In the spiritual realm, there is also a cord that must be cut—the cord to any belief systems from the past that hinder our new life in Christ. We cannot move into the future and receive our proper inheritances if we are holding on to old ways of life. We need to cut away any ungodly belief systems that are feeding us spiritually and, instead, receive life from the breath of God and His words only.

When Israel left Egypt, it was the proper time for her cord to be cut. Israel resisted this, however, and as a result her people did not enter into their inheritance. Only two men of faith, Joshua and Caleb, crossed over into the Promised Land. They led an entirely new generation into Canaan; the old generation died in the wilderness.

The blood within the umbilical cord is known as "cord blood." Medical procedures now use cord blood cells for bone marrow transplants. This is extremely interesting because bones represent structure. Spiritually, when God cuts a cord to the past, He is restructuring our lives, our churches, our businesses, our families—indeed, everything that concerns us.

Christ's blood is now our source of life. Taking a covenant meal—Holy Communion—reminds us of the tremendous sacrifice Jesus paid with His own blood: We have been bought with a price. We belong to Him because He has purchased us.

The Ezekiel passage makes clear that many of us miss this and face painful issues—particularly issues of abandonment and rejection—because of old ties to the past. The child's umbilical cord was not cut; the child was never washed or covered (wrapped in cloth). Because of this rejection, the baby did not feel pitied (he felt that no one cared). This opened the door for deep wounding, and the child was receptive to abandonment issues—never feeling loved, nurtured and protected. Shame becomes a stronghold when a child is raised with these feelings.

## Cutting Free from Generational Iniquities

Along with personal strongholds, we often have to cut ourselves free from generational strongholds and ungodly patterns from the past. If you have ongoing issues that you cannot overcome, it is quite possible that a sinful, iniquitous act from a past generation is connecting you like an umbilical cord to a past belief system, and needs to be cut.

We see this in the passage from Ezekiel 16. In this allegory, the father was an Amorite and the mother a Hittite. Reference to these ungodly heritages is a picture of generational iniquity.

The name *Amorite* is a Hebrew name meaning "a mountaineer, a talker or a slayer." If we place the devil's words above God's words, then Satan has a seated position, or a higher place. And if we heed Satan's words, then he can easily slay us.

Is the enemy talking to you? Are you listening? As a result, does the enemy have a high place in your life? In other words, does Satan have any seated position over you?

The name *Hittite* is a Hebrew word meaning "an annoyer, dread or fear." The word *annoy* means "troublesome or bothersome." There are many different forms that the spirit of fear will attempt to manifest in order to annoy us and cause us dread.

Do you have a dread of your future? Does fear have a seated position in your life? Are you worried by fear of failure, fear of abandonment, fear of death or fear of rejection? What continues to bother or trouble you?

Think further. Have you ever felt that you are simply continuing to "go around the same mountain again"? Are you confronting the same past issues over and over, and find yourself unable to discern the cause? This is a good indicator of generational issues; the word *generation* implies a continuing cycle or circle.

Another indicator of generational issues is the use of the word *always*. Have you said, "Well, I have *always* been this way. I can't change! It will *always* be as it is now."

Most modern-day prophets agree that the Church today is in a spiritual season in which God is exposing old belief systems. God is declaring that it is time to cut yourself free from old patterns and behaviors—whether they are based on your own sins or your generational heritage. I want to go into my promised land; how about you? In order to do so, we must be determined to cut ourselves free from doubt and unbelief, religious mind-sets, generational strongholds and whatever else so easily besets us.

Is anything holding you captive? Do you have trouble moving forward in faith? Are you holding on to the past? Is your spirit challenged to move forward and cross over into your destiny?

Dear one, it is time to cut the cords to the past. We must lock on to what God says, digest His words and cross over into our land of promise. Allow God to lead you, and trust in His power and might to bring you into the destiny He has planned for you.

### Cut the Cords and Move On!

Most of us use every ounce of faith and energy attempting to leave a place called "Here" to get to that promised place of "There." As we travel to "There," we go through a season of transition and change. Transition, simply stated, is moving from one place to another.

This implies that in order to arrive "There," we must be willing to let go of the old sinful nature. Our destiny and fulfillment in God requires us to shift out of an old place and enter into the new.

Part of crossing over into the land of promise involves embracing a fresh move of God's Spirit and allowing Him to lead us down pathways that are new and unfamiliar. Will you allow God to cut the umbilical cord to your past so that you can follow Him and cross over?

Here are some steps that will help you cut the cords to the past and move out of the wilderness. (It is okay to take some baby steps through this.) Prayers are given with these steps to help you express your thoughts to God.

- Sit quietly, taking some time to let the Lord speak to you. If there are sins, rebellions or iniquities in your life or the lives of your ancestors that are keeping you tied to Egypt, let God speak them into your heart. List them below.

_____

_____

_____

- Now, repent of each sin.

*Father, I realize that it is now my time to move forward. I recognize that I am still tied to my past. I confess that I have not been fed fully by Your Holy Spirit. I repent for believing lies from the enemy. I repent for each sin You have shown me.* [Name each one you listed above.]

*I ask forgiveness for not only my sins but also the sins of my ancestors. I plead the blood of Jesus over my generations. Cleanse me from all unrighteousness. Thank You for releasing me from any generational strongholds and ancestral curses that have had legal entrance into my life. Thank You for the blood of Jesus and the awesome completed power of the cross.*

*I ask that You sever the umbilical cord to my past. I believe that Jesus Christ was born to destroy the works of Satan, that He died on the cross for my sins and that He sits at Your right hand, so I know that I am in right standing with You.*

*I choose to believe what Your Word says concerning me, my family and anything else in my life (business, ministry, etc.). I choose to digest only Your Word. I will feast upon Your words of life in the days to come.*

- Close your eyes and imagine yourself as a baby who is about to take his first step on his own. One step, two steps, three steps . . . and now you are moving forward. You did it! Although you may have to stabilize yourself with the nearby coffee table or someone's hand, you have now cut the cord to the past. You have conquered your fear of the unknown. Did you see yourself grabbing a hand along the way? Jesus is there to help you through this process. List below the fears you faced as you let go.

_____

_____

_____

- What victories will you gain as you remove yourself from that old place of fear, doubt and unbelief? List them below.

_____

_____

_____

- Are there any relationships that hold you back? How do they influence you to remain in old patterns of behavior? What are your plans to "let go"? List these below.

_____

_____

_____

- By listing below the very best things that will happen if you fully let go, you will gain vision for your future. List your future steps for the best!

_____

_____

_____

- Take some time to read Luke 18:28–30. Pray and meditate over what Jesus said about letting go.

_Father, I receive my new measure of life today. Thank You for the blood of Jesus that washes me white as snow and cleanses me from past mistakes and all unrighteousness. Today I thank You that I am connected to You. I am fed daily by You and Your Word. In Jesus' mighty name, Amen!_

# — 9 —

# CROSSING OVER INTO THE PROMISED LAND

"So I have come down to rescue them from the hand of the Egyptians and to bring them up out of that land into a good and spacious land, a land flowing with milk and honey."

Exodus 3:8

Have you ever been on a blind date? My husband and I met on one, so I am very happy that I committed to that experience! But what if one of us had backed away from the date because we had not "seen the territory" first?

I am sure the Israelites wondered what the Promised Land looked like. At the time they were to enter it, Joshua and Caleb were the only ones who had actually been there. The rest of the nation had to move forward on a promise, wondering what a land "flowing with milk and honey" could possibly be. They had no photographs, no *National Geographic* televised specials to entice them. They had to trust the Lord.

Moving forward is more than just finding the place called "There." The Lord brought His people to the land of their inheritance, but they had to make the decision to cross over to the other side. Crossing over into our land of promise involves obedience when we cannot see what lies ahead. Yet, as we submit to God's leading, He helps us continue the steps toward our inheritances.

Deuteronomy 28 describes the many blessings God gives us as the result of obedience:

> "If you fully obey the Lord your God and carefully follow all his commands I give you today, the Lord your God will set you high above all the nations on earth. All these blessings will come upon you and accompany you if you obey the Lord your God:
>
> You will be blessed in the city and blessed in the country.
>
> The fruit of your womb will be blessed, and the crops of your land and the young of your livestock—the calves of your herds and the lambs of your flocks.
>
> Your basket and your kneading trough will be blessed.
>
> You will be blessed when you come in and blessed when you go out.
>
> The Lord will grant that the enemies who rise up against you will be defeated before you. They will come at you from one direction but flee from you in seven.
>
> The Lord will send a blessing on your barns and on everything you put your hand to. The Lord your God will bless you in the land he is giving you."
>
> Deuteronomy 28:1–8

How can we possibly fail if we are obedient to the word of the Lord? The Lord is speaking to all of us in this season, directing us to cross over into the wonderful inheritance that is ours because of Jesus' sacrifice. He also has instructed each of us to leave the past behind, remove our old garments and put on a mantle of authority. We must embrace change.

God has good things planned for us! Victory has already been promised through the power of Jesus' blood. As we enter the land that flows with milk and honey, we will reap a bountiful harvest.

## Oppressed and "Bent"

Crossing over into our promised inheritance begins with trust, and trust comes from knowing God's heart for His people. Quite simply, God wants to deliver us from oppression and lead us into a land of freedom and promise: "The LORD said, I have surely seen the affliction of my people which are in Egypt, and have heard their cry by reason of their taskmasters; for I know their sorrows" (Exodus 3:7, KJV).

The Hebrew word for *sorrows* translates as "grief and pain, both physical and mental." God knows the pain that "Egypt" has caused in our lives. As I stated previously, *Egypt* represents darkness and a narrow place. It also symbolizes oppression. We identify *Egypt* today as "the world." We are to be in the world, but not of (the spirit of) the world (see John 17:16).

Exodus 3:7 also tells us that the Lord had seen the affliction of His people. The Hebrew word for *affliction* is derived from a root meaning "oppression." According to *Strong's* lexicon (to which I refer for many of the definitions in this chapter) it is associated with the behavior of being "bowed down, looking down, troubled, weakened, stooped over, humiliated, shamed and in a weakened state." Can you identify with any of these conditions? If you have felt oppressed by the spirit of Egypt and its Pharaoh (symbolic of a demonic stronghold), then I am sure the enemy has attempted to humiliate and weaken you so that you can no longer look up. The enemy's plan is to keep us so stooped over that we cannot see where we are headed. After all, how can someone who is stooped over and looking at the ground stride boldly into a new destination?

The word *affliction* is linked closely to the word *iniquity*, which has several interesting meanings: "perverse, crooked, bent, twisted and distorted." It is the devil's plan not only to weigh us down emotionally with afflictions, but also to distort our thinking. Once we become "bent" in both our emotions and our thoughts, we can be sure that "bent" or sinful actions will soon follow.

Very often, this pattern leading to "bent" behavior goes unnoticed. Iniquity becomes a part of our lifestyles, and is even passed down through the generations. Any iniquitous patterns stand in our way of full growth, thwarting us in our attempts to seek the light. Like a tree limb that curves around an obstacle in its destined pathway, we are left with a permanent "bend" in our belief systems and behavior.

Iniquity, then, causes us to grow in the wrong direction. We tend to seek alternate paths and lifestyles rather than get delivered from the bent places. Maybe you have lived with bent patterns for so long that you have given up hope for deliverance—or you do not even know you need it. Remember that God heard the cries of the Israelites, His heart was moved toward them and He delivered them from their oppression.

Isaiah 53 is one of my most favorite passages as it describes how Jesus took upon Himself our infirmities and carried our sorrows. Read the passage below and ponder the fact that He was wounded for our transgressions.

> He is despised and rejected of men; a man of sorrows, and acquainted with grief: and we hid as it were our faces from him; he was despised, and we esteemed him not.
> Surely he hath borne our griefs, and carried our sorrows: yet we did esteem him stricken, smitten of God, and afflicted.

But he was *wounded* for our transgressions, he was bruised for our iniquities: the chastisement of our peace was upon him; and with his stripes we are healed.

All we like sheep have gone astray; we have turned every one to his own way; and the Lord hath laid on him the iniquity of us all.

Isaiah 53:3–6, KJV (emphasis added)

The word for *wounded* is often translated *pierced*. This Hebraic word is *chalal* and is connected to the same word *chuwl* meaning "to dance." This means that when Christ was pierced for our transgressions and bruised for our iniquities, we can believe that His heart was anticipating *dancing with joy* because He knew His blood would set us free. In addition, this word is directly connected to words that refer to an *inheritance*.

I recall my dream of preparing to dance with the King, which I described at the beginning of this book. Believer, if you are able to sit still right now without jumping up and down and giving praise to God I would be completely in awe. Oh, how true it is when Scripture states that His joy helped him endure the cross!

[We look] unto Jesus the author and perfecter of our faith, who for the joy that was set before him endured the cross, despising its shame, and hath sat down at the right hand of the throne of God.

Hebrews 12:2, ASV

## Getting Ready to "Cross Over"

Like the children of Israel, we have been oppressed by the spirit of darkness, and we have grieved and suffered shame, sorrow and weakness. But there is a way out. God sent us a deliverer—Jesus Christ. He came to set us free from the oppressor.

Now we must do our part. Yes, dear one, it is time to seek our deliverance. Following are eight initial concepts that we need to understand in order to cross over into our inheritances. These are followed by six steps to take you into your land of promise.

### 1. Put on the New Man

First we must examine our spiritual condition, as this determines our position. Ask yourself: What is your affliction? In what areas of thinking do you have a permanent "bend"? Do you suffer with doubt and unbelief? Do you trust God? Look at this Scripture:

> [Put] off, concerning your former conduct, the old man which grows corrupt according to the deceitful lusts, and be renewed in the spirit of your mind, and . . . put on the new man which was created according to God, in true righteousness and holiness.
>
> Ephesians 4:22–24, NKJV

Are you positioned to leave the past behind? It requires putting off the patterns of the old nature, the old man, which is corrupt, and then renewing your mind to the truth (believing what God states concerning you). When you have done that you will be able to put on the new man.

To become fully empowered to cross over and drive out your enemies, you must position yourself and clothe yourself with the righteousness and holiness of Christ.

### 2. Decide to Cross Over

Now that you have determined to put on the new man, realize that the exit from the old place involves making a final decision to cross over to the other side.

Crossing over to the other side is more than just crossing your Jordan. Although the Jordan is significant in the process of possession, it is not the only place of crossing. Like Abraham and like the Israelites, who faced several crossings as they pursued their promises, we, too, come up against numerous places that we must cross over. There is a Red Sea crossing, a crossing over from fear and anxiety to complete trust in God, a Jordan crossing and many other crossings we face during our lifetimes.

### 3. Expect Miracles and Expansion

In Matthew 14:13–14, we read that Jesus crossed the Sea of Galilee and then healed the sick. Jesus was in a desert place, yet people traveled miles to witness His ministry, and with great compassion He healed them. In the evening, still in the desert place, Jesus fed the multitude with only five loaves and two fish. Amazing! That must be what He meant when He said He would cause a river to flow in the wilderness and a path in the desert. We can expect the same miraculous manifestations when we begin to cross over to the other side.

### 4. Cross Over from Fear

Fear is one of the most powerful strongholds we face today. Fear causes insecurity, and insecurity produces unbelief. When fear is active, we see ourselves as small and ineffective rather than focusing on the majesty of God and believing that all things are possible. When we are ready to move forward into the future, the spirit of fear works against us, bringing fear and doubt and often causing paralysis.

Even Jesus' disciples had to cross over from fear. After feeding the multitudes, Jesus told the disciples to get into the boat and return to the other side. Jesus went to the mountains to pray, and the disciples began rowing.

Suddenly, a storm came and the disciples became fearful. Scripture states that their hearts were hardened because they could not comprehend the previous miracle. It is sad to think that they witnessed such a miraculous event and their hearts remained hard concerning the works of Christ.

> When evening came, the boat was in the middle of the lake, and he was alone on land. He saw the disciples straining at the oars, because the wind was against them. About the fourth watch of the night he went out to them, walking on the lake. He was about to pass by them, but when they saw him walking on the lake, they thought he was a ghost. They cried out, because they all saw him and were terrified.
>
> Immediately he spoke to them and said, "Take courage! It is I. Don't be afraid." Then he climbed into the boat with them, and the wind died down. They were completely amazed, for they had not understood about the loaves; *their hearts were hardened.*
>
> Mark 6:47–52 (emphasis added)

I love how the Lord continues to reach out to us—even when our hearts are hard. The Greek word for *hardened* is *poroo* (pronounced po-*ro*-o), which also means "blind." Often we are blinded to the goodness of God due to our mind-sets and fears. He is forever asking us to trust Him.

As Jesus walked out on the water toward them, the disciples thought He was an evil spirit and were terrified. I believe a spirit of fear was sent to torment them because they had begun to doubt the word of the Lord.

When we are in the crossing-over process, the devil often uses storms to cause us to fear and doubt the word of the Lord. But remember this: When Jesus sends you to the other side, He has every intention of your making it! There is no reason to fear, because His word to us is sure.

Jesus called out for the disciples not to be afraid. Only Peter responded with faith and walked on the water toward Jesus. When the winds became more boisterous, he began to fear again and then to sink. Jesus reached out, caught Peter and spoke to him: "You of little faith . . . why did you doubt?" (Matthew 14:31).

Is this not exactly what occurs in our own lives? We receive a word from God to cross over into our land of abundance, so we get into our faith boat and make headway toward our promise. Then the devil comes, and he huffs and puffs and tries to capsize us. If we respond with fear, we open the door to a spirit of torment.

Dear one, when we get into this place, the only way out of fear is to get out of the boat and walk on the water. The only other choice is to become paralyzed by fear and die in that boat. Let's get out of the boat and walk on some water. If we begin to sink, He will be there to stabilize us. He is with us, helping us keep on crossing over to get to the other side.

His perfect love casts out all fear. Having faith in His love for us causes us to rise up with even greater courage to cross over into our future.

### 5. Remain Positioned before the Throne

Let's look at a different image now. Imagine the throne room where God resides. Now imagine that you are standing before His mercy seat. In order to cross over into our promise, we must meet God face to face. Only in the throne room can we position ourselves not only to see God, but also to hear His words and be led by Him into victory. Isaiah did this. He faced the Lord after he left the old behind (see Isaiah 6).

Moses was also a man to whom God spoke face to face. Moses saw God's glory and was determined never to move forward unless God's presence was with him. Unfortunately, as we have noted, Moses was unable to cross over and experience the land flowing with milk and honey. Although he was a man who experienced the miraculous, who saw God's glory and who was an appointed deliverer, Moses still missed it. He used an old pattern based on how God had spoken in an old season, rather than listening to God's new word to him. Maybe he had developed a bent attitude. His mind-set hindered his entering into his promise.

Because we are made righteous through Christ, we need no longer fear that God will reject us. In confidence, we can come to the throne of grace and meet with God (see Hebrews 4:16). Intimacy in His presence is one of the greatest gifts we have due to the blood of Jesus.

### 6. Get Ready for a New Menu

There is new food for us when we cross over. When the Israelites were in the wilderness, they were fed manna and quail. When they crossed over, however, the Lord changed their menu. They no longer received the nutrients from the old diet. In the Promised Land they were in the care of *El Shaddai*—the name for God that signifies the all-sufficient, the many-breasted One, the nourishing, cuddling character of God. In the same way a baby depends on the mother's milk, the Israelites had to depend completely upon *El Shaddai* in the land of milk and honey.

In the new place—a more intimate place—the Israelites had to spend more time in His presence receiving warfare strategy and depend more on His leading than ever before. Israel had to remain properly positioned at all times to hear His instructions.

Joshua had to remain close to God to hear His divine instructions concerning

- how to rise up, overcome fear and lead an entire nation across floodwaters (all within one chapter!)
- when to cross the Jordan
- where to camp before crossing
- how to trust a harlot
- where to cross
- who was to cross over first
- how many stones to take out of the Jordan to build a memorial
- how to position the priests
- how the priests were to position their feet as they stepped into the Jordan
- what to do with forty thousand people armed for war after they crossed over
- when to stop and circumcise the males
- how to convince the males that God said to circumcise them
- how to shift from his paradigm concerning warfare and relate to the Captain of the Hosts

It is the very same for each of us. As we cross over, we cannot be fed by words of the past. Whatever old patterns fed our behavior must be left on the other side of the crossing. As we move into our place of promise, we are to receive nourishment from the promise. The promise is God's Word; all that He says about us, our circumstances and our condition must become our new diet. He is feeding us new bread. When we cross over, we are in His River of Life. And remember, life is in the blood. It is time to shift out of the "stinking thinking" that has polluted our minds and blocked our breakthroughs.

### 7. Drive Out the Previous Tenants

Have you ever taken honey from a beehive? It is war! If you want the fruit from "Beeland," you need a special strategy, and you must put on special military equipment to fight those devilish bees. They are fierce and determined. They understand the importance of unity; they swarm in mighty multitudes. It is not even clear who the real leader is during an attack; they are all one and in one accord. They do not care who gets the medal of honor—they just want to defend their hive!

The devil is not going to allow us to cross over into our land of promise without a fight. Like the beekeeper taking honey from bees, we need a special strategy, and we must be equipped. We cannot go forward into our new place of milk and honey with old armor and old strategy. Old methods of warfare will not suffice. But first, we must understand who our enemies are and the strategies they use.

We can be thankful that God gives us insight into our enemies and their tactics. In Exodus 3:8 the Lord said there were numerous "-ites" in the land: Canaanites, Hittites, Amorites, Perrizites, Hivites and Jebusites. I visualize these "-ites" as demon-like termites that eat away at our foundations.

God said we are to "go in and possess the land." The word translated *possess* actually means "to take the land promised to us by driving out the previous tenants." King David put on the ephod and sought the Lord before battle. We also must seek the Lord for the strategies needed for this season.

Let's look closely at these enemies that block our growth. As you study the names of these "-ites" given below, see if you can recognize some of these strongholds in your own promised land. It might be possible that some have caused your bent behavior. In order to gain victory in your new place, you might have to remove yourself from iniquitous patterns. You might have to kick out of your life the old, established tenants who claim squatters' rights.

These are only a few of the "tenants" that are mentioned in Scripture, but these are the ones of which the Lord spoke directly. (For more information concerning the "-ites" in the land, read *The Costly Anointing* by Lori Wilke [Destiny Image, 1991].) As you read through each "-ite" that may be in your own promised land, remember that you have been bought with a price—the precious blood of Christ. Remain focused on these key verses as you continue to read:

Those who are led by the Spirit of God are sons of God. For you did not receive a spirit that makes you a slave again to fear, but you received the Spirit of sonship. And by him we cry, "Abba, Father." The Spirit himself testifies with our spirit that we are God's children. Now if we are children, then we are heirs—heirs of God and co-heirs with Christ, if indeed we share in his sufferings in order that we may also share in his glory.

Romans 8:14–17

### CANAANITE

This name means "to be subdued and brought low." According to Cornwall and Smith's *Exhaustive Dictionary*, my reference source for the meanings of the names in this section, it means literally "to press down or humiliate." We all can identify times when we have felt humiliated and pressed down or depressed. The anointing of God's Spirit can empower us to rise above our circumstances and defeat and conquer this enemy. Again, when we remember who we are in Christ, the enemy can no longer cause us to feel "less than." Keep in mind that you are a child of the King. We are not slaves but sons and daughters of God.

### HITTITE

This name means "causing dread and fear." Have you ever been terrorized? Maybe you have suffered from anxiety or even had anxiety attacks that paralyze you. I often wonder how many of us miss out on our promised land because of fear. This stronghold caused the entire camp of Israel to miss its destiny.

Fear is the direct opposite of faith. God mentions the words *Fear not* in Scripture 365 times—once for every day of the year. We need not fear because He promises to send His presence before us into battle. According to Romans 8:14–17, we need no longer fear because we are sons and daughters of the King. Remembering that and reminding the enemy of our promises will drive out that Hittite stronghold.

### AMORITE

This name means "a talker and a slayer," which implies a false voice speaking against us, an accuser or even a false prophecy. The enemy will prophesy lies to you. He will speak exactly the opposite of what God has said concerning you and your future. We must discipline ourselves not to listen to his lies. We must be careful to set a watch over our speech, taking care not to speak negatively. We must not murmur and complain. Discipline your mind to think only on what is true, noble, right, pure, lovely and of a good report (see Philippians 4:8). Discipline yourself to renew your mind consistently; this will remove bent thinking. We can silence the voice of this talking spirit by reminding him that he was defeated at the cross by the *finished* work of Jesus.

## PERRIZITE

This name means "a squatter, open and without walls." It implies an unwalled city and a lack of self-discipline, both of which open a person's life to constant bombardment from the enemy. If we do not establish a watch over our speech, our thinking processes and our ears, then we will give the enemy squatter's rights in our lives. If we are consistent to discipline ourselves, however, then we will experience victory on a daily basis.

Thank God that, as King, He has complete reign of His Kingdom. Since we are heirs, we are divinely protected. Let's rise up and command any squatters to leave our land of promise.

## HIVITE

This name means "declarer, pronouncer, one who lives in a village." It is similar to the name *Amorite*, but since it is a villager-type stronghold, it "lives" with us. I consider this stronghold to be a "familiar spirit," which is a demonic spirit often assigned to us at birth.

The word *familiar* means "to be well acquainted with, closely intimate or personal, or pertaining to a family or household." This spirit is like family, and over time we trust its voice. Many times we do not recognize its influence upon our lives and thought patterns. It can speak to us easily, and we will not challenge its voice because it is such a familiar sound. This type of spirit is one of the most seductive and dangerous.

The witch of Endor, whom King Saul sought concerning his future, had a familiar spirit (see 1 Chronicles 10:13–14). In disobedience and rebellion, Saul removed himself from hearing God's voice. As a result of an ungodly "need to know," which, as I stated earlier, opens the door to witchcraft, he

opened himself to ungodly counsel, and died for his trans-
gression. A familiar spirit is closely connected to a spirit of
divination, so we must be careful to guard against the enemy's
false prophecies and lies.

### JEBUSITE

This name means "to be polluted and trodden down." This
is another stronghold that implies depression and oppression.
This name also implies defilement. King David conquered
the Jebusites when he took the stronghold of Jebus. He later
renamed the city Jerusalem, which means "double peace."

The enemy has robbed us of our peace and joy by oppressing us. Through Christ Jesus we have been given perfect
peace. God's peace drives away all fear and anxiety, along
with depression. Our royal inheritance promises us peace—
not peace that the world gives, but peace that can come only
from God (see John 14:27).

### 8. Remember to Advance Patiently

The Israelites did not conquer their enemies all in one day;
the Lord drove them out little by little. So please be patient
as you go into spiritual warfare and drive the enemy from
your territory.

> The LORD your God will drive out those nations before you,
> little by little. You will not be allowed to eliminate them all
> at once, or the wild animals will multiply around you. But
> the LORD your God will deliver them over to you, throwing
> them into great confusion until they are destroyed.
>
> Deuteronomy 7:22–23

Realizing that God goes before us to defeat our enemies
helps us to be more patient for our complete healing and

deliverance. He is a faithful God, and He will perform all He has promised. When Christ went to the cross and shed His precious blood, the enemy was fully defeated. We will face giants in our land, but Jesus has already defeated them on our behalf.

Though we are responsible to drive the enemy out, we are confident that we are fighting *from* the victory and not *for* the victory. We have been made *alive together with Him*. He cancelled our debt of sin by nailing it all to the cross. Colossians 2:13–15 describes how Jesus made a public display of the enemy by His sacrifice:

> When you were dead in your transgressions and the uncircumcision of your flesh, He made you alive together with Him, having forgiven us all our transgressions, having canceled out the certificate of debt consisting of decrees against us, which was hostile to us; and He has taken it out of the way, having nailed it to the cross. When He had disarmed the rulers and authorities, He made a public display of them, having triumphed over them through Him.
>
> Colossians 2:13–15, NASB

Dear one, when we fully believe His Word, when we embrace all that He is and who we are in Him, then we are actively crossing over into our new season and we are possessing our inheritance. The land of promise represents an actual spiritual place. We enter into that new land when we allow Him to be the structure of our lives, businesses, ministries and families. When we give Him full control, then we can possess every promise.

## Steps to Take to Cross Over into the Promise

Are you ready to take the next steps to leaving the wilderness behind and cross over into your promised land? Speak these six steps as prophetic declarations, and then stand up and declare your freedom.

### 1. I renounce . . .

Take some time to renounce any area of unbelief, sin, addiction and false belief. Renounce any bent behavior or thinking. Look over the negative effects of the "-ites" and renounce any areas that resonate with you.

### 2. I acknowledge . . .

Acknowledge the truth. Begin to speak what God has declared concerning you. You might want to gather written prophecies and speak the prophetic words aloud to confirm God's perfect will. Acknowledge that Jesus died for your sins and that His blood cleanses you from all past iniquity.

### 3. I forgive . . .

Words and actions of others can cause deep wounds and rejection, which hinder our future. List the names, if possible, of those whom you need to forgive, including yourself. Remember to name spiritual authorities, teachers, governmental figures, etc.

### 4. I submit . . .

Submit to the plan of God for your life, to legitimate spiritual authority and to the Word of God.

### 5. I take responsibility . . .

Take responsibility for your choices in life. Then develop a disciplined lifestyle, and be determined to blame others no longer for your mistakes or for your situation.

### 6. I disown . . .

Make a decision to disown the sins of others, generational sins and your own sins. Place the sins on the cross and allow the blood of Jesus to cleanse you from your past.

## The Power of a Prophetic Declaration

Declarations have tremendous power. Remembering that life and death are in the power of your tongue, make this prophetic declaration concerning your future:

> I declare that I am moving past all generational sins and strongholds and that I remove myself from all bent behavior. I realize that God has a plan and a purpose for my life. He has a land of promise that awaits my possession, and I declare that no demon will stop me from taking my territory. I declare that no hindrance from my past will stop me from moving forward and fulfilling my destiny. I declare that God has provided a river in the desert and a way out of my wilderness. God has His very best planned for my life. Amen!

Now, precious one, cross over into that land that is flowing with all of God's blessings. Press past every obstacle that attempts to stand in the way of your victory. You are in right standing with God. He has gone before you and defeated all of the "-ites" in your territory. The land is yours!

# — 10 —

# OUR SPIRITUAL
# WEAPONS

Now that you have taken your land of promise, you need to know how to protect it. In other words, believer, we are at war! We are involved in a conflict that spans our universe—the heavens and the earth.

The battle is best described as one between God's forces of good and Satan's forces of evil. Satan is pictured throughout Scripture as a dragon, murderer, thief, liar and serpent. I have written books on his different names, such as "Antichrist" and "Accuser of the Brethren," and how he manifests in a threefold cord of the evil principality Jezebel and her two cohorts, Athaliah and Delilah. To put it simply, Satan opposes God. As the spirit of Antichrist, he opposes Christ, the cross and the revelation of the power of His blood. Ultimately, the devil comes to steal, kill and destroy.

But there is good news! Through Jesus' death on the cross, He defeated Satan on our behalf. There are two aspects we must grasp concerning Satan's defeat. First, Christ made it possible for us to receive God's complete forgiveness for our sins. Second, Christ made it possible for us to receive God's righteousness by faith without having to continue to observe the Law.

Wow! Think about that just for a minute. We are righteous—not because of the Law or being perfect or doing enough religious acts—but through the righteousness of Christ. Because of this fundamental truth, Jesus deprived our enemy of his most destructive weapon against us—guilt. Guilt always recognizes the justness of judgment and punishment. Therefore, dear one, we need to realize that Jesus was punished for our sins. He took our punishment upon Himself at the cross. There is now no more condemnation because of the shed blood of Jesus. As we abide in Jesus, we hold on to the inheritance He has given us. We fight the battle with a clear and steady conscience.

## Our Spiritual Weapons

God has given us spiritual weapons to use against our enemy. In 2 Corinthians 10:4 we read that "the weapons of our warfare are not of the flesh [they are not physical or material], but divinely powerful for the destruction of fortresses" (NASB). Now you understand that you have spiritual weapons to defeat the enemy. These weapons we have are powerful—but remember that they are *powerful through God*. We must depend upon Him completely as we use these powerful weapons. Our victory has nothing to do with us, our own righteousness or self-works. It is the very power of God Himself that causes these weapons to be powerful.

Because of the blood of Jesus, we are never on the defensive in our battle with Satan. There is no need to wonder where or when Satan may strike. We have our spiritual weapons readily available. Remember, Christ lives in us. He is always available to empower us in battle.

The enemy will lie to us as we attempt to lay claim to our spiritual inheritance. He will say such things as:

"You're too weak."

"You don't have a positive testimony."

"You are unworthy to possess anything God has for you."

If we believe these lies we will back away from the battle. We must stand on the fact that we have the victory because of the blood. Let me be completely honest with you: There are many times I *do* feel weak and back away. And at times I still attempt to battle Satan in my own strength. This is, of course, futile. I cannot fight the enemy without realizing the power of the blood of Jesus and what He accomplished through His death and resurrection.

I have to heed these words of Paul continually:

But God chose the foolish things of the world to shame the wise; God chose the weak things of the world to shame the strong. He chose the lowly things of this world and the despised things—and the things that are not—to nullify the things that are, so that no one may boast before him. It is because of him that you are in Christ Jesus, who has become for us wisdom from God—that is, our righteousness, holiness and redemption. Therefore, as it is written: "Let him who boasts boast in the Lord."

1 Corinthians 1:27–31

It always amazes me how God has chosen the least likely and most unworthy people to overthrow Satan's kingdom. I am reminded of so many in Scripture who said to the Lord,

"Who, me?" I am one of those who say, "God, You've got to be kidding! You want *me* to do *what*?" Our confidence must never be in ourselves. We have weapons given to us by God and through God.

So, what are they? In this chapter we will discuss five crucial weapons. All of them are related to the blood of Jesus.

## The Three-Strand Cord

In the book of Revelation, the apostle John identifies a three-strand cord that acts as a powerful weapon against Satan.

> Then I heard a loud voice in heaven say: "Now have come the salvation and the power and the kingdom of our God, and the authority of his Christ. For the accuser of our brothers, who accuses them before our God day and night, has been hurled down. They overcame him by *the blood of the Lamb* and by *the word of their testimony*; they did not love their lives *so much as to shrink from death*.
>
> Revelation 12:10–11

Please make this note: They *overcame* Satan. The blood of the Lamb and the word of testimony are complementary weapons. When they are combined with obedience to God whatever the cost, the enemy cannot win.

*Testimony*, according to Hebraic translation, means "do it again." God wants to bless us and give us victory again and again. He wants to heal our sicknesses and diseases. He wants to free us from bondage and deception. God wants to prove His faithfulness to us. Every time we give a testimony concerning God's goodness, we release a declaration into the atmosphere and cause that atmosphere to become "pregnant" for the miraculous—so that He can bring forth that miracle again!

Psalm 107:2 says this concerning our testimony: "Let the redeemed of the LORD say so, whom He has redeemed from the hand of the enemy" (NKJV). We need to declare continually what God has done for us. We need to say boldly, "I am redeemed from the hand of the enemy." When we do this, it is a weapon against Satan. Ephesians 1:7 reminds us, "In him [Jesus] we have redemption through his blood, the forgiveness of sins, in accordance with the riches of God's grace."

Notice two things provided by the blood: forgiveness of sin and redemption. Giving testimony to that fact reinforces the power of the blood. We must give personal testimony and say, "Through the blood of Jesus all of my sins are forgiven, and through that blood I have also been redeemed from the hand of the enemy."

I find that many believers do fully understand the power behind giving testimony as to what God is doing and has done. Revelation 19:10 states that "the testimony of Jesus is the spirit of prophecy" (ASV). For years I taught that this referred to prophecy as a demonstration of the Spirit. While that is true, it means more. This passage declares that our testimonies prophesy what God still desires to do. In other words, when someone gives testimony of his healing, he is testifying to the fact that Jesus desires to heal again. A testimony says, "Do it again, Lord!" How wonderful is that?

But please understand the personal commitment involved here. We hold high our weapons in this battle even unto death. We must revere God's goodness more than our own lives. This is a crucial decision we must all make.

So allow me to make this simple. We overcome Satan when we (1) declare what the Word says concerning the blood of Jesus; (2) testify from personal experience what God says through His Word; and (3) give ourselves to Him fully in service. Using all three of these together—*the blood of the Lamb, the testimony of God's goodness and death to self*—makes our warfare supernaturally effective against our enemy.

We need to be reminded continually that Jesus became our Passover Lamb. Peter states that fact:

> For you know that it was not with perishable things such as silver or gold that you were redeemed from the empty way of life handed down to you from your forefathers, but with the *precious blood of Christ, a lamb without blemish or defect.* He was chosen before the creation of the world, but was revealed in these last times for your sake.
>
> 1 Peter 1:18–20 (emphasis added)

Remember, on Passover night the blood of a lamb was applied to the homes of the Israelites. The father in each family killed a lamb and collected its blood in a basin. Then, he dipped a hyssop branch in the blood and sprinkled it on the doorposts and lintel. The blood thus applied protected the family.

Hyssop is common in the desert, growing among rocks and along walkways. It has long branches, making it easy to hold—maybe that is why the soldier offered Jesus liquid to drink in a sponge attached to a hyssop branch. Hyssop was also used medicinally for ulcers and cleansing lepers. By understanding the uses of hyssop, we see that the blood and its application through this plant go hand in hand.

For us today, I believe our hyssop is our testimony. When we give testimony concerning the power of the blood of the Lamb, it is as if we are dipping into a basin of blood and applying it over the hearts of God's people. We overcome the enemy by the blood of the Lamb and the word of our testimony and loving not our lives unto death.

## Cleansing from Sin

The next vital weapon in this battle to hold our inheritance is cleansing from sin. First John 1:7 testifies of the cleansing power of the blood: "But if we walk in the light, as he is in the light, we have fellowship with one another, and the blood of Jesus, his Son, purifies [cleanses] us from all sin."

Actually, one of the first results of being reconciled with God through the sacrifice of Jesus is this cleansing from sin. The blood of Jesus exercises spiritual power in the soul. As believers, and knowing that the blood is fully effective in our lives, we each can become a new person. The blood's power begins to transform us and our old nature leaves. We become a new creation when we are in Christ. Lusts, perversions, ungodly lifestyles and more are cleansed and subdued because of the power in the blood. Even subconscious sins lose their power! I like to describe *being cleansed* as "being delivered from the pollution of sin and its power."

In the Old Testament, cleansing was necessary for each individual sin. In the New Testament, cleansing depends solely on Jesus and His never-ending intercession (see Hebrews 7:25). Believer, when we understand these truths, we can live with confidence knowing that at every moment we are being cleansed and protected by the power of the blood.

Never forget that the enemy does not want you to be free and cleansed. He will continually speak lies concerning your righteousness through the blood of Jesus. The battle is won by remaining steadfast in your testimony and confession—knowing in your heart that you have been redeemed.

And remember also that the battle is many times simply in your mind! Remember to cast down those imaginations and bring every thought into complete captivity when the enemy attempts to keep you clothed in garments of shame (see 2 Corinthians 10:4–6).

## Justification

The next vital weapon for our warfare is the fact that we can defeat voices of condemnation because we are justified by the blood. Romans 5:8–10 explains this clearly:

> But God demonstrates his own love for us in this: While we were still sinners, Christ died for us. Since we have now been *justified by his blood,* how much more shall we be saved from God's wrath through him! For if, when we were God's enemies, we were reconciled to him through the death of his Son, how much more, having been reconciled, shall we be saved through his life!
>
> (emphasis added)

The key phrase in this passage is *justified by His blood.* Both *justify* and *justification* are key New Testament words. By studying the word *justify*, we find that it means "to make righteous, to acquit from sin and to hold guiltless." I find it interesting that one of the Hebrew definitions used for *justify* is the word *cleanse.* I like to describe being justified as being made righteous through the blood of Jesus and being held completely guiltless for our sins. It is as if we had never sinned. Because we are justified by Jesus, we are completely clean.

Second Corinthians 5:21 says that God made Jesus "who had no sin to be sin for us, so that in Him we might become the righteousness of God." Dear one, at the cross, Jesus became sin. He took upon Himself our sinfulness, assumed the penalty for our sins and took the judgment for every sin we have committed.

Jesus paid the full price of redemption. Only in Christ are we made righteous—we can work hard at trying to be righteous, but it will not make us righteous. We might try to pray more, fast more and attend church more to be righteous, but works will not make us holy and righteous. No, only God's righteousness makes us righteous. Jesus never knew sin; He was pure and spotless. God allows us to take on His righteousness through faith.

This is the testimony that you need to say when the enemy lies to you and says that you are guilty of sin and that you deserve to suffer and be punished:

> Through the blood of Jesus I am justified and made righteous. I can look in the mirror and see myself cleansed from my past. I can see myself as if I had never ever sinned! Therefore, I can stand before God without shame or guilt. I need not fear that He will reject me, because when the Father sees me, He sees the blood that covers me. The stain of sin has been removed. I am not going to battle the enemy based upon my own righteousness, but with the righteousness of Jesus Christ and the power of His precious blood!

## Sanctification

A little earlier I wrote about cleansing as a vital provision for our warfare. *Cleansing* has mostly to do with our old life and the stain of sin that is removed due to the blood of Jesus.

*Sanctification*, on the other hand, is a provision that helps us in the battle where the new life is concerned. It means being set apart and becoming transformed into His likeness. The Lord has always made it clear that His people are set apart from all others on earth. *Sanctification* actually means "union with God." It means *holiness*.

Sanctification expresses the fullness of blessing purchased through the blood of Jesus. Whenever you are tempted by the enemy to doubt that you are set apart and being transformed daily, say this as part of your testimony:

Because of the blood of Jesus, I am sanctified. I am set apart and made holy. The enemy, Satan, has no power over me and has no claim against me. This includes curses of any type, infirmities and iniquities. I am completely washed clean by the blood.

## The Eternal and Continuing Plea

There is one more weapon that needs to be mentioned concerning the blood of Jesus and our warfare. Hebrews 12:22, 24 states, "You [all true believers] have come to Mount Zion . . . to the sprinkled blood that speaks a better word than the blood of Abel." In the heavenly Mount Zion, the blood of Jesus was sprinkled in the Holy of Holies on the mercy seat before the very presence of God.

What does this mean? There is a parallel in Scripture that can help us understand this. After Cain had murdered his brother Abel, Scripture says that Abel's blood cried out to God from the ground (Genesis 4:10). Since Abel had been murdered, his lifeblood cried out for vengeance. The blood of Jesus sprinkled in heaven is also crying out—not for vengeance (though Christ was also murdered), but for mercy. This is why His blood was sprinkled on the mercy seat—to give us God's mercy.

Mercy is huge for us! Mercy, put simply, is God's loving-kindness toward each of us. No matter what we have done, He still loves us. Mercy gives us a picture of God's unconditional love. His willingness to forgive everyone who asks Him was accomplished once and for all when Jesus' blood was sprinkled upon heaven's mercy seat.

Once we have personally given testimony to our faith in Christ and the power of His blood, we are eternally forgiven of all sin and receive His mercy. The blood of Jesus is speaking continually on our behalf in the presence of God. Each time we fail, we need to remind ourselves that we are righteous in God's eyes because of the blood. Each time we are tempted, anxious or fearful we need to remind ourselves that the blood of Jesus is speaking on our behalf right now—in God's holy presence. By doing this, we deprive Satan of a major weapon he uses against us—guilt and condemnation.

Because of the blood we are empowered to live in victory.

# — 11 —

# HIDDEN IN CHRIST

For [as far as this world is concerned] you have died, and your
[new, real] life is hidden with Christ in God.

Colossians 3:3, AMPLIFIED

As you move into your land of promise, it becomes increasingly important to remain properly positioned in His divine presence. This is a position of staying "hidden" in Christ, covered by the protection of His blood.

In the New Covenant, everything should emerge from a sense of knowing who we are in Christ. This question of identity is a major battle in our minds. Remember discussing strongholds? Let's review this. A stronghold is any thought, belief or imagination that opposes God. Second Corinthians 10:5 describes a *stronghold* as "the thoughts that attempt to rise up against the knowledge of God." This includes mindsets or belief systems that oppose the truth of God. In other words, when the enemy lies to us concerning our identity and we do not cast down the thought or belief connected to that lie, it can become a stronghold.

God desires for us to be partakers of His glory. Colossians 1:27 reminds us that "God was pleased to make known what is the riches of the glory of this *mystery* among the Gentiles, which is Christ in you, the *hope of glory*" (ASV, emphasis added).

I emphasized the word *mystery* because we began the first chapter by discovering hidden mysteries concerning our royal inheritances. These mysteries have been held—waiting for the set time to be revealed to you. Stand up and declare this statement: "This is my set time to possess my royal inheritance!"

Now let's look at the word *glory*, which is connected to the word *reputation*. It becomes clear that as Christ lives in us, we are empowered to take upon us His reputation. In other words, we have Christ and all of His glory within us—living in us at all times. When we are in a spiritual battle we need to remind the devil of that.

When we received Jesus as our Savior, He came to live in us—we became His temple. It amazes me that He chooses to live inside of me. I could imagine fabulous temples I might choose to live in—but Jesus chooses to live in us. What a humbling thought!

## We Are Hidden in Christ

Let's take a look at another related passage of Scripture so that we can better understand the freedom of this new life in Christ:

> Since, then, you have been *raised with Christ*, set your *hearts on things above*, where *Christ is seated* at the right hand of God. Set your *minds on things above*, not on earthly things. For you died, and your life is now *hidden with Christ* in God.

When Christ, who is your life, appears, then you also will appear with him in glory.

Colossians 3:1–4 (emphasis added)

We have looked at a number of passages concerning life in Christ and the inheritance He gives us, but the key aspect is that we are "hidden."

The word *hidden* is the Greek word *krupto* (pronounced *kroop*-to) and is a verb meaning "to conceal, hide or keep secret by covering." This means that when we are covered by the blood, we are hidden in Him. There are several significant benefits for us in this place of new life.

First is safety. The devil cannot locate us when we remain "hidden" in Jesus. I look at it this way: We are in such a secret place the devil cannot touch us. What a safe place to be!

Second is empowerment. Being hidden in Christ assures us of power, authority and dominion. The verses above say that we have been "raised" with Christ. This refers not only to resurrection from the dead and eternity with Jesus, but also to the fact that we have been "raised up a level" and are empowered to defeat the enemy. We are seated with Christ in heavenly places—we have a seated position of victory.

Third is intimacy. Our new life is "hidden" in Christ. Think about that special place in Christ a minute—hidden away in Him. To be hidden means that in this special, tucked-away place that is both private and intimate, He covers us with His wings and hides us in Himself. As we dwell there, we develop a passion to understand the mysteries of God.

Fourth is blessing. As we seek Him in this intimate place, He promises to repay us. I believe that part of His reward is opening up to us realms of revelation and understanding. In the secret place, God reveals His secret plans and gives us His heavenly strategies to overcome the enemy.

The Ancient of Days desires to speak to each of us in the secret place and unveil many mysteries from days past along with ancient strongholds that affect us.

> He who dwells in the *secret place* of the Most High shall abide *under the shadow* of the Almighty. I will say of the LORD, "He is *my refuge* and *my fortress*; my God, in Him I will trust." Surely He shall deliver you from the snare of the fowler and from the perilous pestilence. He shall *cover* you with His feathers, and *under His wings* you shall take refuge; His truth shall be your shield and buckler. You shall not be afraid of the terror by night, nor of the arrow that flies by day, nor of the pestilence that walks in darkness, nor of the destruction that lays waste at noonday. A thousand may fall at your side, and ten thousand at your right hand; but it shall not come near you. Only with your eyes shall you look, and see the reward of the wicked.
>
> Psalm 91:1–8, NKJV (emphasis added)

We, as believers, must remain hidden under His wings. In that hiddenness, we are divinely protected from our enemies and given counsel for godly living. We can also be kept free from the fear of any false covering.

Let's look next at the danger of false coverings. We are susceptible to these if we choose to step out from under His wings.

### The Occult Spirit Defined

The main purpose of an occult or occultic spirit is to "cover" us with lies and deceit. When I speak of an occult spirit, I am referring to a demonic spirit with a specific assignment to hide truth and revelation from us. Satan assigns his demons to specific tasks with different assignments. This evil spirit works to lead us into deception and to seduce us to believe lies.

Let us examine the word *occult* in order better to understand how the enemy uses it to "cover" us in this way.

First, according to *Webster's* the word *occult* means "a system claiming to use knowledge of secret or supernatural powers." Satan attempts to twist and distort the mysteries and secrets—the revelation—of God. Because the Body of Christ is receiving greater levels of revelation today, we must be sure we are listening to the correct voice.

Another definition of *occult* is "secret, undisclosed and hidden from view." This implies that the enemy will keep revelation hidden from us. The word *revelation* means that "something once hidden becomes known." The words *occult* and *revelation* are closely connected, and we must be extremely discerning as we make advancements into deeper revelation.

In other words, Satan schemes and places snares in front of us so that we will stumble, become confused and heed the wrong voice while uncovering mysteries. There is a distinction between the "mysteries" of God and the "mysterious." The occult spirit entices us with the "spooky and mysterious." Although at times God is mysterious, He protects His mysteries until He reveals them to His prophets.

One further definition of *occult* is "to block or shut off from view, to hide." Again, the enemy's assignment is to block our view and keep the truth of God hidden from us. He blinds us with circumstances and mountains that seem to stand in our way. If we do not discern the source of this attack, our minds become confused, our bodies become weak and we are unable to see our way.

Precious one, the devil is a liar and a deceiver. He tries to hinder our ability to see properly and to disable our ability to receive God's revelation. Satan also twists truth and distorts vision to get us to align with his lies, by which he brings us under his false covering.

When I speak of a "false covering," I am referring to times when we are not following the leading of our true Shepherd. Where Christ leads, we must follow. Psalm 91 gives us a clear description of the Lord and how we are protected under His shadow. The passage goes on to paint a lovely picture of Him as our fortress (our protection) and how He covers us with His wings, sheltering us from sickness, disease and the snares of the enemy.

Precious believer, when we trust in the Lord and His words, realizing we are covered also by His protective blood, we can have confidence that we are safely hidden in Christ. If, however, we believe what Satan declares concerning us, it is just the same as taking off our righteous garments and exchanging them for garments of shame. This is why occult spirits attempt to hide truth. Satan wants to cover you with his lies!

## Occult Spirits Conceal Demonic Activity

Another purpose behind an occult spirit is to conceal the demons blocking our breakthroughs. If we can be blinded successfully to their activity, we will not be able to determine the stronghold behind the difficult situation we are facing.

Here is an example. My husband battled kidney failure symptoms, fatigue and heart-related pain for months. Yet when he underwent a multitude of tests, his heart appeared to be normal. No doctors could find the cause for his medical condition.

As I prayed, my spiritual discernment spoke loudly that these physical ailments were manifestations of a serious heart condition. Finally, we insisted on one more medical procedure, which included a hospital visit. I called our intercessors to pray against an occult spirit that causes things to remain hidden and masked. We prayed and fasted for three days.

That final test revealed that he had three main blockages in his heart! He was scheduled immediately for triple bypass heart surgery. He is doing well today, but if it had not been for God exposing what was hidden, he might have died.

Thank the Lord for revelation! As we stay hidden in Christ, God's Spirit of revelation—one of the sevenfold Spirits of God—will reveal demonic activity and give us wisdom to battle these occult spirits.

## The Hidden Things Can Cause Fear

As we walk into our inheritances, God establishes a new plan, a new order. But we can often be fearful of the new thing. Fear can lure us out from the shelter of His wings. We must remind ourselves that we are hidden in Christ and covered by His blood in order to overcome this tool of the enemy.

When Moses died, the Lord told Joshua to rise up, cross over the Jordan and lead the people:

> After the death of Moses the servant of the LORD, it came to pass that the LORD spoke to Joshua the son of Nun, Moses' assistant, saying: "Moses My servant is dead. Now therefore, arise, go over this Jordan, you and all this people, to the land which I am giving to them—the children of Israel. Every place that the sole of your foot will tread upon I have given you, as I said to Moses. From the wilderness and this Lebanon as far as the great river, the River Euphrates, all the land of the Hittites, and to the Great Sea toward the going down of the sun, shall be your territory."
>
> Joshua 1:1–4, NKJV

The old had to die in order for the Lord's plans and purposes to be seen. Moses—the old order—was dead. Now a new order was being established. Joshua was instructed to leave the past behind and embrace the challenge ahead.

But Joshua faced fears as he stepped up to the plate. He was told by the Lord three times to be strong and of good courage and not to fear: "Have I not commanded you? Be strong and courageous. Do not be terrified; do not be discouraged, for the LORD your God will be with you wherever you go" (Joshua 1:9). The Lord told Joshua that there was no need to fear his future or the giants in the land because He would be with him in the journey.

Like Joshua, every one of us faces fear when moving into the unknown. But God is with us. He does not desert us. "He guides me in paths of righteousness for his name's sake" (Psalm 23:3).

Joshua is an example of how to remain properly aligned with God's purposes, especially during seasons of change and transition. He pressed through fear and intimidation. He remained obedient as he led God's army across the Jordan and into unfamiliar territory. Although there were many giants in the land of promise, Joshua remained stable and full of faith. He allowed God's Spirit to cover him so that the spirit of fear could not, and he subsequently led God's army into a season of possession.

## King Saul's Disobedience and Fear

In contrast to the powerful, faithful example of Joshua stands King Saul—a prime example of a self-centered, disobedient leader. Saul felt he had a better way than God and forfeited his destiny because he rejected the Lord. Whereas Joshua led God's army into a season of possession, Saul led his army into a season of regression and spiritual depression. Joshua led the Israelites forward into their future; Saul led them backward because of his own disobedience. Joshua's leadership was a catalyst of resolve and resolution; Saul's leadership was tainted with selfishness, fear and rebellion.

Under Saul's leadership, the Israelites began to fear their enemies. Instead of facing the Philistines, they ran and hid among rocks, caves and thickets. Can you imagine? The Israelites were on a roll. They had been favored by God in battle and had collected the spoils. But suddenly a spirit of fear overtook their faith.

Remember: The occult spirit promotes a demonic force of hiddenness. If we fear, then the enemy attempts to overshadow us with torment and cause us to run and hide. As a result, we open doors for other occult spirits to occupy our minds, and we open ourselves to the enemy's lies and deception. Fear, then, causes us to hide and prevents us from moving into the next level of God's glory.

Let's not be like Saul and the Israelites and fear our enemies. God says, "The one who is in you is greater than the one who is in the world" (1 John 4:4). We must be on guard as we move forward and gain new territory. We must have faith in His power to overcome rather than succumbing to fear that our own power will not be enough. Only in this way will God's glory be more fully manifested in us.

## Don't Hide from God; Hide in Him

As we leave behind old paradigms, old belief systems, we begin to shake our personal "government." What has governed our lives in the past will be shaken so that God can establish a new order in our lives. The Lord desires to be the one who directs our steps and, thereby, ensures our victory. He plans to release us to a new measure of victory and authority. Let's study more closely what happened to King Saul so that we can understand how to shift out from the old and establish the new in our lives.

As 1 Samuel 13 begins, Saul had reigned over Israel for two years and he was about to lead Israel into battle against the Philistines, but Saul failed the test when he was measured by God.

In Saul's army were three thousand men. Two thousand were in the city of *Michmash* (meaning "hidden") and in the hill country of Bethel, and another thousand were with Jonathan in *Gibeah* (meaning "high place") of Benjamin. Eventually the people were called together in *Gilgal* (meaning "a wheel rolling," indicating cycling). These names offer spiritual insight into many positive attributes of the people of God.

On the positive side we could say that God's children were in a "high place" in God, seated in heavenly places. They were safely "hidden" away in this secret place with divine protection. From such a place, they could "cycle" or roll out of any wilderness mentality and defeat their enemy. This is how the Israelites should have seen themselves.

But on the negative side, the Israelites, led by Saul, chose to be defiled in their thought processes. Rather than focusing on the positive attributes of God's ability to fight on their behalf, they focused on the fact that the Philistines had thirty thousand chariots, six thousand horsemen and as many people as the number of the sands. Talk about feeling overwhelmed by the odds!

The name *Philistine* means "to wallow in the dust" and represents defilement. Battling against the Philistines defiled the Israelites' faith and determination. An occult stronghold grasped them, and they chose not to remain "hidden in God," but instead ran and tried to hide themselves:

> When the men of Israel saw that they were in a strait, (for the people were distressed,) then the people did hide themselves

in *caves*, and in *thickets*, and in *rocks*, and in *high places*, and in *pits*.

1 Samuel 13:6, KJV (emphasis added)

Have you ever run and hidden because you were afraid? The enemy attempts to make us run to places that appear safe but are really places of great danger because occult spirits have established strongholds there.

These places where the Israelites hid give us spiritual insight into the snares of the enemy. One of the translations for the Hebrew word for *cave* means "naked and ashamed." If we run to a cave, we will end up completely vulnerable to the enemy. Isolation in a cave is dangerous. We must remain connected to the Body of Christ and remain accountable to spiritual authority. To separate from accountability is to become vulnerable to deception.

One of the translations of the word *thicket* means "hook." The enemy desires to hook us to the past. The enemy wants to chain us to our past responses of fear, doubt and unbelief.

*Rocks* represent anything in our lives that is a foundation other than Christ. Jesus is the only Rock, and anything else is shaky ground. We cannot depend upon any natural foundation, such as money, possessions or relationships. Jesus Christ is our only sure foundation.

One of the translations of the word for *high places* is "cliffs" and is rooted in the words *battle cry* and *roar*. Do you know that the enemy has a false roar? When a lion's pride is left alone while the male hunts for food, there is the threat that another lion will enter and seize control of the pride. A false authority can enter into the camp and roar over them. Yet it is a false roar—one not given from the lion in true authority. The lion's pride must be well trained to hear and discern the true roar.

Likewise, we also must be careful that we do not come running out at the sound of a false roar. A false roar would be a false sense of security—maybe the security of a past relationship or a past belief system.

The word translated *pit* means "dungeon and prison." If we run and hide anywhere other than God, we become open prey to a demonic lockdown. If we remain in a defiled place, we will remain in a spiritual prison.

Dear one, it is time to leave old hiding places and stay close to the Lion of Judah!

## God's System of Testing

While the Israelites were in the wilderness, they faced challenges continually, such as the daily need for water and food. Just one day without food is enough to make most of us irritable, so I cannot imagine how difficult it was to have faith for food and water year after year in the desert. God was using their natural surroundings to test them, and the Israelites' response was not good: They were fearful, hungry, thirsty and weary. They began to murmur and complain.

God was so angry with their response that He was tempted to destroy them many times. But, ultimately, God's period of testing worked. At the end of forty years, God had a new generation of great potential. They measured up! So He empowered Joshua and a new group of warriors to cross over.

If God were to test you right now on your ability to remain safely hidden in Him, what would He find? Would He say that you are complacent in the face of temptation? Would He say that you are compromising with the lies the devil offers? Would He say that you are afraid to let go of your past and move forward?

When I was a child, my mother would get out her yardstick and measure my growth. I will bet you had marks on your wall, too. It is an exciting thing as a child to look at those marks and see how we have grown. God wants us to look and see how we have grown. He wants us to be blessed. And He wants to give us more of His glory.

Remember: The occult spirit is determined to place false authority and false covering over us. Its main assignment is to wear us down so that we finally relent and make covenant agreement with the lies.

Jesus Christ has come to set us free. There is a way out from the old. He has made a way for us—a way in the wilderness and a river in the desert. We must run to His secret place.

# — 12 —

# ESTABLISHING YOUR
# VICTORY STRUCTURE

In [Jesus] the whole building, being fitted together, grows into
a holy temple in the Lord, in whom you also are being built
together for a dwelling place of God in the Spirit.

Ephesians 2:21–22, NKJV

It's beautiful! I love the design. This is going to be a gorgeous house. The kitchen has a wonderful flow pattern for traffic. The family room is spacious. It is just perfect!" I was poring over a set of construction plans. My husband and I were building our very first home, and I was elated.

Not everyone gets as excited about blueprints as I do, but I have been exposed to the home-building business since I was a teenager. My parents were successful homebuilders for more than forty years, and I grew up around the fresh smell of sawdust. It was always my dream to build a home.

(I wonder if the Father gets as excited as He builds His tabernacle within us.)

After our final approval of the construction plans, the foundation was prepared and poured. The foundation generally does not look like much—just a sheet of gray concrete. But a proper foundation is very important because the entire house rests upon that mixture of rocks and other materials. All the more reason for the Lord to take His time laying foundations for the human tabernacles He chooses to live in.

I was ready for the next stage—the framing—so that I could actually see something happening. I looked forward to the lumber shaping every wall, beam and roofline. In the natural, seeing walls erected is so inviting. When we can actually *see* progress, there seems to be, at that point, a type of supernatural synergy that develops—vision!

Although I love decorating a home, the framing part of building is still my favorite. The framers came early, and by the time I arrived, several walls were raised. *How exciting!* I said to myself. *Walls! (Walls in a good way, I mean.)* I remained on the jobsite for hours watching the framing crew continue to erect the walls. They chalked off every room, measured the lumber, sawed each piece and then—*rooms!* Several days later the framing was completed, the roof was on, and we began the interior work on the home.

The process of building a home can be compared to the process of building our spiritual lives. How are our spiritual homes built? Most of the time we focus on the foundation— and rightly so—but the framework is also important because it is the part that holds the house together. Our spiritual houses need to be built upon the solid Rock of Christ Jesus. But we also need to look closely at our framework (see Luke 6:48). Let's take a few moments to consider this.

## What Is Our Framework?

If we were to take snapshots of our lives today and lay those photographs over the blueprints of our hopes and dreams, we might be surprised to see how different the actual framework really is. In other words, what failures, setbacks and challenging cycles of life have hindered us from walking into our inheritances?

Allow me to ask you a question, as we are coming to closure on our journey together. Have you been able to identify thought patterns that oppose your divine royalty through the blood of Jesus? Do you see any beliefs that still hinder you from receiving your promised royal inheritance through Christ?

One thing about royals, they know their history. They rehearse the records of their ancestry and understand their lineage. The connection to their past gives them purpose to do something significant during their reign. Since we rule and reign through Christ, it is important to know what has been historically recorded—in other words, to study the Word and claim the same promises for ourselves.

Ask yourself, "What does my structure consist of?" Are you experiencing the fullness that you desire? Are you experiencing the victory God promised? Do your prophetic words declare breakthroughs that you have not experienced? Do you have a testimony? Can you develop one?

If you have answered no to any of these questions, then it is time for you to shift from an ungodly structure of defeat into God's victory structure. It is time for you to go before God and receive fresh strategies from His throne for your life.

God sees everything from a state of completion. At the time of Creation, He framed the entire universe with invisible words (see Hebrews 11:3). At the very instant we were created in our mothers' wombs, He formed and fashioned us after

His own image. God had a plan, a structure, a framework that He spoke into existence. His plan was a picture of our future that was framed in heaven.

But the enemy came into our lives and sowed his demonic seeds of lies and deceit into our hearts. As a result, our belief systems became defiled and we developed religious paradigms that limit God and His ability to heal and restore us. Rather than believe that we are chosen, loved and accepted, we believe that we are abandoned, rejected and unloved. As a result of our pain, we have made many wrong choices and our lives are framed with hopelessness and despair.

God wants to restore us and empower us to fulfill our destinies. He wants each of us to know that He has not abandoned or forsaken us. He is the Great Physician and the Great Restorer of hopes and dreams. The Lord declared through the prophet Joel, "I will restore to you the years that the swarming locust has eaten, the crawling locust, the consuming locust, and the chewing locust" (Joel 2:25, NKJV). It is God's heart's desire to restore all that has been lost and destroyed.

God brings the unseen into existence. When He created the universe, it was unseen and then became visible. As He restructures your life, the very same will happen for you.

Fear not, O land; be glad and rejoice, for the LORD has done marvelous things! Do not be afraid, you beasts of the field; for the open pastures are springing up, and the tree bears its fruit; the fig tree and the vine yield their strength. Be glad then, you children of Zion, and rejoice in the LORD your God; for He has given you the former rain faithfully, and He will cause the rain to come down for you—the former rain, and the latter rain in the first month. The threshing floors shall be full of wheat, and the vats shall overflow with new wine and oil.

Joel 2:21–24, NKJV

The prophet Joel is declaring a new structure of victory. God will release the latter rain and the spring rain together in the very same month, meaning that you will experience the flood of His power and anointing. He is going to overflow your life with the new wine, and your barns will be full.

## Building Victory Structures

We have discussed the fact that we are the temples of God and that the Spirit of God lives in us. Take a moment and study the following passage. Notice that we were bought with a price—that price was the blood of Jesus. And Christ Jesus has chosen to live in us.

> Or know ye not that your body is a temple of the Holy Spirit which is in you, which ye have from God? and ye are not your own; for ye were bought with a price: glorify God therefore in your body.
>
> 1 Corinthians 6:19–20, ASV

In studying a *victory structure* for possessing our inheritance, I believe we need to consider how to protect the temple in which Christ lives. Guarding our hearts, being imitators of Christ and remaining in the Word will build our faith and protect the temple of the Lord, right? But let's consider the fact that we are children of the King and have been chosen as His "royal" temple. This gives us all the more reason to develop a victory structure in our lives to continue to possess our royal inheritance.

It is time to look beyond our past experiences of failure, grief and loss, and see ourselves as royalty with opportunities to rule and reign. We cannot see this with our natural eyes; we must look to our future with supernatural vision. If we are created in God's image, we also can speak to the invisible and declare it to become visible. We can frame our world, build a holy temple, with words that God has declared and, therefore, experience a new structure of victory. Never let your enemy rob you of shifting into your new victory structure!

### Victory Structure #1: Ask God to Overshadow You

Let's take a look at the story of Esther. This remarkable story shows how God positioned a young Jewish woman to save an entire bloodline and receive her royal inheritance.

When Esther's people were being threatened with annihilation by Haman, the Amalekite, her cousin Mordecai reminded her of the Jewish destiny. Mordecai said that the deliverance and enlargement God had promised would surely come, but unless Esther stepped into her unique place in the palace and begged King Ahasuerus for mercy, neither she nor her descendants would witness it.

Esther must have realized that her moment to make a difference in history had arrived. Although she most likely had not planned for her life to take this particular direction, Esther saw destruction coming—and her unique, strategic position to try to stop it.

Her response was a three-day fast, asking God to cover and protect her, as she prepared herself (her personal temple). Esther then laid down her life and approached the king. (This is also a good example of trusting the fact that when we die to self we remain *hidden* and *covered*.)

She received favor—the king extended the royal scepter to her—and her request was granted. The Jewish people were given the right to take up arms and protect themselves from their enemy. The Jewish people were successful in the battle, and the curse of death and destruction from Haman, the Amalekite, was broken.

Esther and Mordecai then wrote a decree that every generation would remember:

> These days should be remembered and observed in every generation by every family, and in every province and in every city. And these days of Purim should never cease to be celebrated by the Jews, nor should the memory of them die out among their descendants.
>
> Esther 9:28

This season of remembrance established by Esther and Mordecai was named Purim. The Feast of Purim is celebrated each year in the months of March and April, which align with the Hebrew month of Adar. In a Glory of Zion International Ministries newsletter (March 25, 2006), Chuck Pierce teaches that the word *Adar* means "the pregnant month," a spiritual time to conceive the plans and purposes of God.

There is spiritual significance in this celebration for Christians as well. The Feast of Purim reminds us that we are in a season when our spiritual womb is being prepared for enlargement. A supernatural pregnancy involves the Lord overshadowing each of us with His glory. Like Esther, we must have faith that God has given us abundant favor, and then we can begin to walk in that new measure of godly favor.

Two evil structures threatened Esther and might have kept her from receiving her inheritance. One was fear of death. Esther knew the law: Approaching the king without being summoned by him meant immediate death. The only exception was for the king to extend the golden scepter to the individual, granting pardon. Esther literally laid down her life for the destiny of her people.

The second death structure was already in the making. It was a literal structure—the gallows—with a hangman's noose awaiting. Haman had ordered the construction of the gallows in order to hang Mordecai.

Precious saints of God, the enemy has also plotted against each of us. He eagerly awaits our destruction. The same two death structures await us today, spiritually speaking. But if we choose to die to self and embrace the advancement of the Kingdom of God, as Esther did, we can be empowered to walk in our full potential and achieve our destiny—and the Kingdom of God will be advanced. By drawing a bloodline against the enemy, we are ever more empowered to defeat any opposing spirit that seeks to steal our inheritance.

### Victory Structure #2: Defeat and Overthrow Death Structures

Esther defeated the death structures not only by laying down her life for the benefit of the Kingdom, but also through divine favor. This awesome level of favor was given to Esther because of her character.

When Esther was brought into the harem of the king, she endured twelve months of sacrifice and purification before being presented to King Ahasuerus. (Again, Esther was preparing her temple for God's destiny in her life.) Twelve is the symbolic number of government. As a result of her dedication to purity, she was empowered to walk into a governmental position in which she was given power to reverse a decree of death against her, her household and the entire Jewish nation.

As modern-day Esthers, we, too, must endure a period of separation. If we also lay down our lives, develop a Kingdom mentality and allow the Lord to purify our motives, then it is possible that the same ability to reverse decrees of death will be given to each of us. Remember: Christ in us is our hope of glory. His living in us will defeat death structures. We must pray over our prophetic words and promises and do warfare. We must obtain favor with the King by separating ourselves from the world, obeying Him and laying down our lives.

As part of her purification, Esther bathed in myrrh. Myrrh is bitter to the taste but has many healing qualities. To receive divine empowerment to overthrow death structures, we cannot skip the myrrh season. It will not be over in just one day; we must endure the bitter experiences, allowing the Lord to heal our hearts and settle us firmly into His divine plans.

Myrrh was also the oil used to prepare bodies for burial. Once more, we recognize how valuable it is to die to self and selfish ambition in order to gain godly power and authority on this earth.

Esther's Hebrew name was *Hadassah*, meaning "myrtle." The myrtle is an evergreen tree and its leaves, flowers and berries were used as perfume. Her name represents the beauty and fragrance we must carry with us as we approach the King to gain favor. As a result, we, too, will be able to break demonic structures of death and release life to our circumstances.

### Victory Structure #3: Seek the King and His Kingdom

Esther's twelve months of preparation put her in position to approach the throne at a crucial point of her nation's history. Esther changed her culture. Because of her faith and the favor she obtained, the Jewish people moved out of a death structure into a structure of blessing and expansion.

To receive our inheritances, we must realize that our plans for our future must include His plans for our future. In fact, His plans must become priority. We must go into the throne room and seek His heavenly strategies for our lives. If we, like Esther, are determined to lay down our own agendas and seek the King, then we can leave once and for all an old structure of bondage and live in a structure of victory.

Esther's time of separation prepared her for the future and allowed her people to overthrow the decrees of Haman, the Amalekite. The Amalekites were notorious for preying on the weak and feeble. They would lie in wait behind moving camps and pick off the weak ones who lagged behind. Those who moved slowly were either murdered or robbed and taken into slavery. We cannot be slow in moving forward. We must decide today to follow God's leading. Seek Him and His Kingdom. Your faithfulness to remain in His secret place before the throne and to continue to seek His heavenly strategies will keep you in the River of Life.

Seek Him, and you will find Him. If you knock at heaven's door, He promises that heaven will open for you. You cannot experience heaven without receiving His promises. God will extend His scepter to you, just as King Ahasuerus did for Queen Esther.

### Victory Structure #4: Decree a Thing and It Shall Be Established

When we make a decree, the Word of God says it becomes established: "Thou shalt also decree a thing, and it shall be established unto thee: and the light shall shine upon thy ways" (Job 22:28, KJV).

In other words, the decree can become a foundation upon which to build. Many of us are attempting to build our future, but we are not coming into agreement with God's Word. This means that we are not decreeing what God has already spoken concerning the situation.

Satan has devised a plan of destruction against us. Many of us have battled the spirit of death and aborted dreams since the time of our births. We can reverse every decree the enemy has made concerning our lives, however, by writing a new decree.

Because Esther walked in the king's favor, he gave her permission, as I have noted above, for the Jews to defend themselves against the Amalekite invasion. She wrote a new decree, and it released the entire Jewish nation from a death assignment:

> King [Ahasuerus] replied to Queen Esther and to Mordecai the Jew, "Because Haman attacked the Jews, I have given his estate to Esther, and they have hanged him on the gallows. Now write another decree in the king's name in behalf of the Jews as seems best to you, and seal it with the king's signet ring—for no document written in the king's name and sealed with his ring can be revoked."
>
> Esther 8:7–8

We also can write a new decree, which will reverse the curse of death. Just like Esther, God is giving us the same opportunities to write a decree concerning our finances, health, children, houses or whatever concerns us. We can reverse the enemy's old decrees that have framed our world and write a new decree, and God will seal it.

## Your New Decree

Dear one, I encourage you to take some time to pray and write a decree. Get real with God. Getting up close and personal with the Father will ensure that your decree is from a pure motive. Pour out your heart to Him, and let His Spirit guide you while you write a new decree over your life. Then believe God to reverse every curse of death. Keep in mind that you are already royalty and you have the power to declare a royal decree.

Here is an example of a written decree. (Remember: This needs to be in your own words.)

*Father, I realize that the devil has decreed death and destruction over my life. I have battled* [for example: *a spirit of poverty and hopelessness*] *for a very long time. I believe it began from the time I was born. Since I was a child, I have battled* [for example: *fear and anxiety*]. *I realize that this is not what You have decreed over my life. You have stated in Your Word that I am called and chosen. Your Word states that I am the head and not the tail. I receive a new measure of faith today. I decree that I will no longer* [for example: *be fearful*] *because I am trusting in You. In the name of Jesus, I repent of being in covenant with the words of Satan, and I believe that I am loosed from captivity. I am being established and positioned for Your abundance according to Your divine purpose. In Jesus' name, Amen.*

When Jesus was in the wilderness and Satan tempted Him, Jesus replied to His enemy with these words: *It is written.* Now that you have written your decree that reverses the curse of death and destruction, tell the devil, "It is written," and enter into your new measure of victory!

## Your Royal Possession

For a very long season we have been experiencing God's *chronos* time—the natural time, the daily "grind" of life. In *chronos* time, we go through our normal daily activities, believing and hoping for the *kairos* time—the exact moment when a supernatural change will occur and we will be launched into our promises.

Well, dear one, this is the season for you to shift into your next season of *royal possession* by declaring the power of the blood of Jesus. It is your time to enter God's throne room and see His heavenly strategies for your life. It is your time to plunder the enemy's camp and take back all that was stolen. It is your time for every promise of breakthrough and blessing to be unveiled.

Many of us have lived in the past for so long it is still in the framework, or structure, of our lives. It is time for this to change. We are in a *kairos* time now. We must do what it takes to shift out of ungodly structures of defeat into God's victory structure.

Think of it this way. God is a God of judgment, yet His judgment involves His divine mercy. At the cross, mercy was applied to all of us. When we abide in Jesus, God judges sin by releasing divine forgiveness. He judges sickness and disease by releasing divine healing. Christ's blood cries out for the Father to judge all that the enemy has put upon us—disease, sin, pain, sorrow, grief—with His mercy. Hebrews 12:24 says this: "Jesus [is] the mediator of a new covenant, and [His] sprinkled blood . . . *speaks* a better word than the blood of Abel" (emphasis added).

When Abel's blood "cried out," it was a call for help. Lexicons tell us that the Hebrew word used is *tsa'aq*, and words connected to this type of crying out mean "to cry out in distress and need, to make a clamor, to be summoned, to cry aloud in grief and to call together." Here we can make a direct connection to the blood of Jesus still speaking. By examining the crying out of Abel's blood and comparing it to Christ's blood, which is still speaking, let's ask ourselves this question: *What is Christ's blood still speaking?*

Christ's blood cries out to those in distress, to those in need and grieving.

His blood offers a better covenant of healing and deliverance through one complete sacrifice.

215

His blood makes a clamor in the camp of the enemy.

His blood stirs up the angels in heaven to war for the victory of the saints.

His blood summons believers to His holy mountain and into His divine presence.

His blood draws the hosts of heaven together to war on our behalf.

His blood declares that our inheritance was set in stone when the stone was rolled away.

His blood speaks full delivery of a promise, royal inheritance realized.

Hallelujah!

Dear reader, it is time to cross over into your fulfillment. Let God's framework, based upon the finished work of the cross, be the structure that holds up your life. Make this confession today: "I am crossing over!"

Receive God's heavenly strategies. Cross over into your promise. I will see you on the other side.

**Sandie Freed** and her husband, Mickey, are the founders and directors of Zion Ministries in Hurst, Texas. Together they pastored a local church in Texas for fourteen years, and today they apostolically oversee the Zion Kingdom Training Center. Sandie is an ordained prophetess with Christian International Ministries and travels extensively teaching prophetic truths to the Body of Christ. Sandie and Mickey also travel nationally and internationally as the Christian International IMPACT Team, in which they apostolically and prophetically oversee regions and churches for their network.

Sandie has written numerous books, including *Destiny Thieves: Defeat Seducing Spirits and Achieve Your Purpose in God*; *Conquering the Antichrist Spirit*; and *Breaking the Threefold Demonic Cord*. She is a featured guest on television and radio, where she shares her testimony of God's healing and delivering power. A gifted minister in dreams and visions and spiritual discernment, Sandie is a sought-after speaker and seminar instructor for her insight on dreams and visions and discerning demonic strongholds over individuals, churches and regions.

Sandie and Mickey, along with daughter, Kim, and son-in-law, Matt, are active ordained ministers with Zion Ministries.

For more information, contact Sandie at

Zion Ministries
P.O. Box 54874
Hurst, TX 76054
(817) 284–5966 or (817) 589–8811 (office)
email: Zionministries1@sbcglobal.net
website: www.zionministries.us

# More Insight from Spiritual Warfare Expert Sandie Freed

**To learn more about Sandie and her books, visit zionministries.us.**

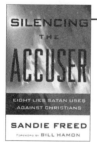
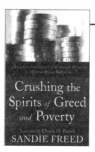